Study Guide Part 2: Chapters 8–10

To Accompany

Accounting Principles
Fifth Canadian Edition

JERRY J. WEYGANDT Ph.D., C.P.A.
University of Wisconsin—Madison

DONALD E. KIESO Ph.D., C.P.A.
Northern Illinois University

PAUL D. KIMMEL Ph.D., C.P.A.
University of Wisconsin—Milwaukee

BARBARA TRENHOLM M.B.A., F.C.A.
University of New Brunswick—Fredericton

VALERIE A. KINNEAR M.Sc. (Bus. Admin.), C.A.
Mount Royal University

Prepared by
JERRY P. ZDRIL B.Sc., C.G.A.
Grant MacEwan University

JOHN WILEY & SONS CANADA, LTD.

Copyright © 2010 by John Wiley & Sons Canada, Ltd.

Copyright © 2009 by John Wiley & Sons Inc. All rights reserved. No part of this work covered by the copyrights herein may be reproduced or used in any form or by any means—graphic, electronic, or mechanical—without the prior written permission of the publisher.

Any request for photocopying, recording, taping or inclusion in information storage and retrieval systems of any part of this book shall be directed in writing to The Canadian Copyright Licensing Agency (Access Copyright). For an Access Copyright Licence, visit www.accesscopyright.ca or call toll-free, 1-800-893-5777.

Care has been taken to trace ownership of copyright material contained in this text. The publishers will gladly receive any information that will enable them to rectify any erroneous reference or credit line in subsequent editions.

Library and Archives Canada Cataloguing in Publication
Zdril, Jerry
   Study guide to accompany Accounting principles, fifth Canadian edition, Jerry J. Weygandt . . . / Jerry Zdril.

ISBN 978-0-470-67666-0 (pt. 1).—ISBN 978-0-470-67852-7 (pt. 2)

   1. Accounting—Problems, exercises, etc.
   I. Title.
HF5636.A33 2009a Suppl. 1   657'.044   C2009-906920-2

Production Credits
Acquisitions Editor: Zoë Craig
Vice President and Publisher: Veronica Visentin
Vice President, Publishing Services: Karen Bryan
Creative Director, Publishing Services: Ian Koo
Editorial Manager: Karen Staudinger
Editorial Assistant: Sara Tinteri
Marketing Manager: Aida Krneta
Typesetting: Thomson Digital
Cover Design: Natalia Burobina
Printing & Binding: EPAC Book Services

Printed and bound in the United States
1 2 3 4 5 EPAC 14 13 12 11 10

John Wiley & Sons Canada, Ltd.
6045 Freemont Blvd
Mississauga, ON L5R 4J3
Visit our website at: www.wiley.ca

CONTENTS PART 2

CHAPTER · 8 ACCOUNTING FOR RECEIVABLES   233

CHAPTER · 9 LONG-LIVED ASSETS   263

CHAPTER · 10 CURRENT LIABILITIES AND PAYROLL   303

How to use the Study Guide in this Book

TO THE STUDENT

This study guide will aid you significantly in your study of *Accounting Principles, Fifth Canadian Edition*, by Jerry J. Weygandt, Donald E. Kieso, Paul D. Kimmel, Barbara Trenholm and Valerie Kinnear. The material in the study guide is designed to reinforce your understanding of the principles and procedures presented in the textbook. It is important to recognize that the study guide is a supplement to and not a substitute for the textbook.

This study guide contains the following materials for each chapter in the textbook:
- Study objectives
- Preview of the chapter
- Chapter review of key points
- Demonstration problem and solution
- Multiple choice questions
- Matching exercise for key terms and definitions
- Exercises

Solutions to the review questions and exercises are provided at the end of each chapter to help you assess how well you understand the material. The solutions explain the reasoning behind the answer, so you get immediate feedback as to what, how, and why.

To benefit the most from this study guide, we recommend you take the following steps:
1. Carefully read the chapter material in the textbook.
2. Read the chapter preview and review in the study guide.
3. Take notes in class.
4. Answer the questions and exercises for the chapter in the study guide and compare your answers with the solutions provided. If you answer a question incorrectly, refer back to the textbook for a discussion of the point you missed.
5. Solve the end-of-chapter material in the textbook as assigned by your instructor.

The study guide should help you prepare for examinations. The chapter review points, class notes, and other materials will help you determine how well you can recall information presented in each chapter. When you have identified topics that you need to study further, return to the textbook for a complete discussion.

Suggestions for Effective Studying

Want to get better grades? Read on!

Good students have a system for studying. In the next few pages, we'll give you some guidelines that we think can help improve the way you study—not only in your accounting course, but in every course. If you need more specific help, we suggest you ask your instructor or consult a career counsellor at your school.

How to Use a Textbook

Textbooks often include material designed to help you study. It's worthwhile to flip through a textbook and look for the following:

- **The Preface**. If an author has a point of view, you can find it here, along with notes on how the book is meant to be used.
- **The Table of Contents**. Reading the table of contents will help you understand how the topics covered in the book fit together.
- **The Glossary**. The most important terms and ideas for you to know will be in the glossary, either at the end of each chapter or at the end of the book.
- **The Appendices**. Found at the end of certain chapters, appendices contain such things as:
  - More difficult material.
  - Answers to selected problems.
  - Specimen financial statements.

How to Read a Chapter

Before Class: Skim

Unless you're told to know a chapter thoroughly by class time, it's a good idea just to skim it before class.
- Become familiar with the main ideas so that the lecture will make more sense to you.
- As you skim the chapter, ask yourself if you already know something about the material.
- Note any material that is unclear and listen carefully for explanations of that material during the lecture.

In particular, look for the following:
- **Study Objectives**. These are what you will be expected to know—and be able to do or explain—by the end of the chapter.
- **Chapter-Opening Vignettes**. Each chapter opens with a brief story that reflects the topic of the chapter. The vignette will give you an idea of how accounting relates to your day-to-day life.
- **Boldface or *Italic* Terms**. These are important terms, concepts, or people.
- **Headings**. Read the major headings to see how the material fits together. How are the ideas related to each other? Do they make sense to you?
- **Summary**. A good summary repeats the main points and conclusions of the chapter, but it does not explain them. The summary usually matches up with the study objectives and introduction to the chapter.

After Class: Read

After skimming the chapter and attending class, you are ready to read the chapter more closely.
- **Check for Meaning**. Ask yourself as you read if you understand what the material means.
- **Don't Skip the Tables, Figures, and Illustrations**. These contain important information that may be on a test. They may also offer a different perspective on the material and help enhance your understanding of it.
- **Read the Sidebars and Feature Boxes**. These items are set off from the main text, either in the margin or in colour boxes. They may include real-world examples, amusing anecdotes, or additional material.

- **Review**. Read the chapter again, especially the parts you found difficult. Review the study objectives, chapter introduction, summary, and key terms to make sure you understand them.
- **End-of-Chapter Questions**. Do all of the end-of-chapter questions, exercises, or problems. For the exercises and problems, make sure you have memorized which equations or rules apply and why. Also do any practice problems assigned by your instructor. These problems will not only help you, but show you what kinds of questions might be on a test. If you have trouble with any:
  - Review the part of the chapter that applies.
  - Look for similar questions and do them.
  - Ask yourself which concept or equation should be applied.
- **Use the Study Guide**. After you've read and studied the chapter, use the study guide to identify which areas you need to review in the text.

How to Take Notes

The ability to take notes is a skill, and it is one you can learn. First, here are a few practical tips:
- Arrive in class on time and don't leave early. You might miss important notes or assignments.
- Sit close enough to the instructor so you can hear him or her and read any slides or transparencies.
- If you don't understand something, ask questions.
- Do not read the text during class—you'll miss what the instructor is saying. Listen, take notes, and ask questions.

Now for the note-taking itself:
- **Listen for Ideas**. Don't try to write everything the instructor says. Instead, listen and take notes on the main ideas and any supporting ideas and examples. Make sure you include names, dates, and new terms. In accounting classes, take down all rules, equations, and theories, as well as every step in a demonstration problem.
- **Use Outlines**. Organize ideas into outlines. Indent supporting ideas under the main ones.
- **Abbreviate**. To help you write more quickly, use abbreviations, either standard ones or ones you make up. For example, leaving out vowels can sometimes help: Lvg out vwls can ...).
- **Leave Space**. Leave enough space in your notes so that you can add material if the instructor goes back to the topic or expands a problem later.

How to Use a Study Guide (In General)

A study guide is specific to the textbook you use. It can't replace the text; it can only point out places where you need more work. Here are some tips to help you use a study guide effectively:
- Use it only after you've read the chapter and reviewed your class notes.
- Ask yourself if you really understand the chapter's main points and how they relate to each other.
- Go back and reread the sections of your text that deal with any questions you missed. The text will not ask the same questions as the study guide, but it can help you to understand the material better. If that doesn't work, ask your instructor for help.
- Remember that a study guide can't cover any extra material that your instructor may lecture on in class.

How to Take Tests
Studying for a Test

Studying for tests is a process that starts with the first class and ends only with the last test. It helps to do the following during the entire semester:
- Follow the advice we gave about reading a chapter and taking notes.
- Review your notes:
  - immediately after class. Clear up anything you can't read and circle important items while the lecture is still fresh in your mind;
  - periodically during the semester; and
  - before a test.
- Review audio or video recordings of lectures, if they have been made.

Now you're ready to do your final studying for a test. Leave as much time as you need and study under the conditions that are right for you—alone or with a study group, in the library or another quiet place. It helps to schedule several short study sessions rather than to study all at one time.
- **Reread the chapter(s)**. Follow this system:
  - Most importantly, look for things you don't remember or don't understand.
  - Reinforce your understanding of the main ideas by rereading the introduction, study objectives, and summary.
  - Read the chapter from beginning to end.
- **Redo the problems**. Make sure you know which equation to apply or procedure to follow in different situations and why.
- **Test Yourself**. Cover up something you've just read and try to explain it to yourself—or to a friend—out loud.
- **Use Memory Tricks**. If you're having trouble remembering something—such as a formula or items in a list—try associating it with something you know or make a sentence out of the first letters.
- **Study with a Group**. Group study is helpful after you've done all your own studying. You can help each other with problems or quiz each other, but you'll probably just distract each other if you try to review a chapter together.

(A Note about Cramming. Don't! If you cram, you will probably only remember what you've read for a short time, and you'll have trouble knowing how to generalize from it. If you must cram, concentrate on the main ideas, the supporting ideas, main headings, boldface or italicized items, and study objectives.)

Taking a Test
After giving you some general tips, we'll focus on different types of tests: objective, problem, and essay.
- **Before the Test**
  - Make sure you eat well and get enough sleep.
  - If the instructor doesn't mention what material will be covered or what kind of test it will be, ask.
  - Arrive early enough to get settled.
  - Bring everything you need—bluebook, pens, pencils, eraser, calculator—and the book, if it's an open-book test!
- **As You Begin the Test**
  - Read the instructions completely. Do you have to answer all of the questions? Do certain questions apply to others? Do some questions count more than others? Will incorrect answers be counted against you?

- Schedule your time. How many questions are there? Try to estimate how much time to leave for each section. If sections are timed so that you won't be able to return to them, make sure you leave enough time to decide which questions to answer.
- **Taking the Test**
  - Read each question as you come to it.
  - Answer the easier questions first and go back to the harder ones.
  - Concentrate on questions that count for more marks.
  - Jot notes or equations in the margin if you think they will help.
  - Review your answers and don't change an answer unless you're sure it's wrong.
- **Dealing with Panic**
  - Relax. Do this by tightening and relaxing one muscle at a time.
  - Breathe deeply.
  - If you don't know an answer, go on to the next question.

Objective Tests
(Multiple choice, true-false, matching, completion, or fill-in-the blanks)

- Watch out for words such as "always," "all," "every," "none," or "never." Very few things are always or never so. If a question or answer includes these words, be careful.
- If you are uncertain about a multiple choice answer, try to narrow the choices down to two and make an educated guess.
- On a matching test, match up the easy ones first. This will leave fewer possibilities for the difficult ones.
- Make educated guesses for objective questions. If you really have no idea and a wrong answer will count against you, leave it blank.

Problem Tests
- If an equation is long, jot it down before you work on the problem.
- Remember that math builds one equation on another. If you can't remember a particular equation, try to remember how it was derived.
- Don't despair if you can't figure out what a question is asking. Try to figure out part of it first. If that doesn't work, go on; sometimes a later question will jog your memory.
- If your instructor gives credit for partially correct problems, make sure you include the way you worked out a problem.
- Make sure that your calculator works before the test and, just in case, know how to do the problems without it. Sometimes you can hit the wrong button, so it helps to have a rough idea of what your calculator should be giving you.

Essay Tests
- Write a rough outline before you begin. If that takes too much time, just jot down all the things you want to say and then number them. Organize what you're going to say into groups of related ideas.
- Make a point in each paragraph. The easiest way is to make the point in the paragraph's first sentence and then back it up.
- Use examples, facts, and dates to back up what you're saying.
- Do what the question asks for. If it asks you to compare two things, for example, go back and forth between them; don't spend all your time on one of them.
- If you have no idea what to write, try to remember ideas that your instructor stressed in class and see if you can relate the question to those ideas.
- Check your time. If you're running out, write your last points down without explaining them; your teacher will at least know what you were going to explain.

chapter 8
Accounting for Receivables

Study objectives >>

After studying this chapter, you should be able to:
1. Record accounts receivable transactions.
2. Calculate the net realizable value of accounts receivable and account for bad debts.
3. Account for notes receivable.
4. Demonstrate the presentation, analysis, and management of receivables.

Preview of Chapter 8

In this chapter, we will review the journal entries made when goods and services are sold on account and when cash is collected from those sales. The chapter then covers how companies estimate, record, and, in some cases, collect their uncollectible accounts. We will also learn about notes receivable, and the statement presentation and management of receivables. The chapter is organized as follows:

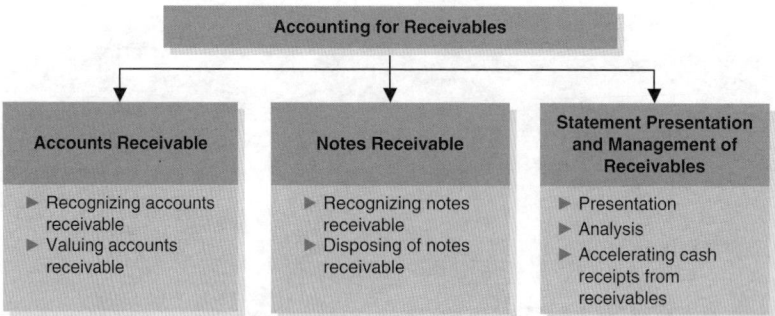

Accounts Receivable

Receivables are claims that are expected to be collected in cash. They are usually due from individuals and other companies. The two most common types of receivables are accounts receivable and notes receivable.

Accounts receivable are amounts owed by customers on account. They result from sales of goods and services. **Notes receivable** are claims for which formal instruments of credit are issued as proof of debt. Notes and accounts receivable that result from sale transactions are also called trade receivables.

Recognizing Accounts Receivable

Study objective 1
Record accounts receivable transactions.

Accounts receivable are recorded when a merchandise company records the sale of merchandise or when a service company records a service provided on account. Accounts receivable can be reduced by sales returns and allowances and sales discounts.

Adorable Junior Garment sells merchandise on account to Zellers on July 1 for $1,000, with payment terms of 2/10, n/30. On July 4, Zellers returns merchandise worth $100 to Adorable Junior Garment. On July 10, Adorable Junior Garment receives payment from Zellers for the balance due. Adorable Junior Garment uses a periodic inventory system.

The journal entries to record these transactions on the books of Adorable Junior Garment are as follows:

Jan. 1	Accounts Receivable—Zellers	1,000	
	Sales		1,000
	To record sale of merchandise on account.		
4	Sales Returns and Allowances	100	
	Accounts Receivable—Zellers		100
	To record merchandise returned.		
10	Cash [($1,000 − $100) × 98%]	882	
	Sales Discounts [($1,000 − $100) × 2%]	18	
	Accounts Receivable—Zellers		900
	To record collection of accounts receivable.		

Subsidiary Accounts Receivable Ledger

A business usually has several, or sometimes hundreds, of customers. If it recorded the dollar amounts owed by each customer in the one general ledger account, Accounts Receivable, it would be difficult to determine the balance owed by any one customer at a specific time. To keep track of each customer, companies use a **subsidiary ledger** for each one.

Each entry affecting accounts receivable is basically posted twice: once to the general ledger and once to the subsidiary ledger. Entries to the subsidiary ledger are posted daily, while entries to the general ledger are summarized and posted monthly.

The accounts receivable general ledger account is the control account. The balance of the control account must agree with the total of the balances in the individual accounts receivable in the subsidiary ledger after posting to the general ledger. The following shows an example of the relationship between the control account and the subsidiary ledger for receivables.

Accounts Receivable is a control account.

GENERAL LEDGER

Accounts Receivable — No. 112

Date	Explanation	Ref.	Debit	Credit	Balance
2011 July 4				100	(100)
31			10,000		9,900
31				5,900	**4,000**

ACCOUNTS RECEIVABLE SUBSIDIARY LEDGER

The subsidiary ledger is separate from the general ledger.

Kids Online — No. 112-203

Date	Explanation	Ref.	Debit	Credit	Balance
2011 July 11	Invoice 1310		6,000		6,000
19	Payment			4,000	**2,000**

Snazzy Kids Co. — No. 112-413

Date	Explanation	Ref.	Debit	Credit	Balance
2011 July 12	Invoice 1318		3,000		3,000
21	Payment			1,000	**2,000**

Zellers Inc. — No. 112

Date	Explanation	Ref.	Debit	Credit	Balance
2011 July 1	Invoice 1215		1,000		1,000
4	Credit memo 1222			100	900
10	Payment			900	**0**

Interest Revenue

At the end of each month, the company can use the subsidiary ledger to easily determine the transactions that occurred in each customer's account during the month. They may send the customer a statement of transactions for the month. If the customer does not pay in full within a specified time, most retailers add interest charges to the balance due.

Finance charges added to an account must be recognized on the seller's books as interest revenue. Interest revenue, when charged to customers on overdue accounts, is included in other revenues in the non-operating section of the income statement. Interest revenue is recorded as an increase to accounts receivable, as follows:

Accounts Receivable	XXX	
Interest Revenue		XXX

Nonbank Credit Card Sales

Debit and bank credit card sales are cash sales (see Chapter 7). Sales on credit cards that are not directly associated with a bank are reported as credit sales. For example, sales using company credit cards such as Canadian Tire are always recorded as credit sales by the company. The amount is receivable from the customer who uses the company's credit card. If that customer had used a bank credit card, the amount would have been recorded as a cash sale by the company.

Transactions and payments can now be processed much more quickly in the electronic environment. If it takes longer than a day or two to process the nonbank credit card transaction and collect cash, it should be treated like a credit sale.

Recall that credit card expenses, along with debit card expenses, are reported as an operating expense in the income statement.

Valuing Accounts Receivable

> **Study objective 2**
> Calculate the net realizable value of accounts receivable and account for bad debts.

Receivables should be reported on the balance sheet as a current asset. Reporting is sometimes difficult because not all receivables will be collected. The **net realizable value** is the amount of the receivables that will be collected. Net realizable value is the amount that should be reported in the financial statements. Using net realizable value for receivables helps to avoid overstating assets and profit.

When receivables are written down to their net realizable value because of credit losses, owner's equity must also be reduced. This is done by recording an expense, known as **bad debts expense** (also sometimes called uncollectible account expense), for the credit losses. If a company waits until it knows the specific accounts that will not be collected, it would end up recording the bad debts expense long after the revenue is recorded.

To record bad debts in the period in which the revenue occurs, the company must estimate the uncollectible accounts receivable. The allowance method is used to estimate uncollectible accounts and match expected credit losses against sales in the accounting period in which the sales occur. The allowance method of accounting for bad debts estimates uncollectible accounts at the end of each accounting period.

The allowance method is required for financial reporting purposes when the amount of bad debts is material (significant). Its three essential features are the following:
1. Recording estimated uncollectibles: The amount of uncollectible accounts receivable is estimated at the end of the accounting period. This estimate is treated as bad debts

expense and is matched against revenues in the accounting period where the revenues are recorded.
2. Writing off uncollectible accounts: Actual uncollectibles are written off when the specific account is determined to be uncollectible.
3. Recovery of an uncollectible account: When an account that was previously written off is later collected, the original write off is reversed and the collection is recorded.

Neither the write off nor the later recovery affects the income statement.

1. Recording Estimated Uncollectibles

The adjusting entry to record estimated uncollectibles is as follows:

Bad Debts Expense   XXX
    Allowance for Doubtful Accounts   XXX
To record estimate of uncollectible accounts.

Bad Debts Expense is debited, and the amount is reported on the income statement as an operating expense. The account credited, Allowance for Doubtful Accounts, shows the amounts that are estimated to be uncollectible in the future.

Allowance for Doubtful Accounts, a contra account to Accounts Receivable, is used instead of Accounts Receivable. With the use of the contra account, the total of the subsidiary account balances remains exactly equal to the control account, Accounts Receivable. Also, the estimate of the uncollectible accounts does not distort the actual amounts posted to Accounts Receivable.

The Allowance for Doubtful Accounts, subtracted from the Accounts Receivable, gives the value of the amount of receivables expected to be received in cash. This is the Net Realizable Value and is calculated as follows:

$$\boxed{\text{Accounts Receivable}} - \boxed{\text{Allowance for Doubtful Accounts}} = \boxed{\text{Net Realizable Value}}$$

Approaches Used in Estimating the Allowance. Companies must estimate the amount of uncollectible accounts. Two approaches may be used: (1) percentage of receivables, and (2) percentage of sales.

Percentage of Receivables Approach. Under the percentage of receivables approach, management uses experience to estimate the percentage of receivables that will become uncollectible. The percentage may be applied to the receivables as a whole, or applied with different percentages to customer balances according to the length of time that they have remained unpaid, using an aging schedule.

This approach improves the reliability of the estimate, providing a better estimate of net realizable value of the accounts receivable.

For example, Manahan Company estimated that 10% of $500,000 in receivables will become uncollectible. Before recording the estimated bad debts, the Allowance for Doubtful Accounts has a credit balance of $20,000.

The estimated uncollectible accounts applied to the receivables as a whole is $50,000 (10% × $500,000). This is the required balance in the Allowance for Doubtful Accounts at the balance sheet date.

The amount of the adjusting entry is the difference between the required balance ($50,000 CR) and the existing balance ($20,000 CR) in the allowance account. The adjusting entry to record the estimated uncollectible accounts for the year ended 2011 is as follows:

Dec. 31	Bad Debts Expense	30,000	
	Allowance for Doubtful Accounts		30,000
	To record estimate of bad debts expense.		

If the allowance account had a debit balance prior to the adjustment, the adjusting entry would still be the difference between the required balance and the existing balance.

For example, assume the Manahan Company estimated uncollectible accounts to be $50,000 and the allowance account has a debit balance of $5,000.

The amount of the adjusting entry is the difference between the required balance ($50,000 CR) and the existing balance ($5,000 DR) in the allowance account. The adjusting entry to record the estimated uncollectible accounts for the year ended 2011 would be:

Dec. 31	Bad Debts Expense	55,000	
	Allowance for Doubtful Accounts		55,000
	To record estimate of bad debts expense.		

Because a balance sheet account (Accounts Receivable) is used to calculate the required balance in another balance sheet account (Allowance for Doubtful Accounts), the percentage of receivables approach is often called the **balance sheet approach**. It is an excellent method of estimating the net realizable value of the accounts receivable.

Percentage of Sales Approach. The percentage of sales approach calculates bad debts expense as a percentage of net credit sales. Management determines the percentage based on past experience and the company's credit policy.

For example, Manahan Company estimates that 5% of its $100,000 net credit sales will become uncollectible. The estimated bad debts expense is $5,000 (5% × $100,000).

The adjusting entry to record the estimate of uncollectible accounts for the year ended 2011 is as follows:

Dec. 31	Bad Debts Expense	5,000	
	Allowance for Doubtful Accounts		5,000
	To record estimate of bad debts expense.		

When calculating the amount in the adjusting entry ($5,000), the existing balance in Allowance for Doubtful Accounts is ignored.

This approach to estimating uncollectibles results in an excellent matching of expenses with revenues because the bad debts expense is related to the sales recorded in the same period. Because an income statement account (Sales) is used to calculate another income statement account (Bad Debts Expense), and because any balance in the balance sheet account (Allowance for Doubtful Accounts) is ignored, this approach is often called the income statement approach.

The illustration below compares the balance sheet approach with the income statement approach.

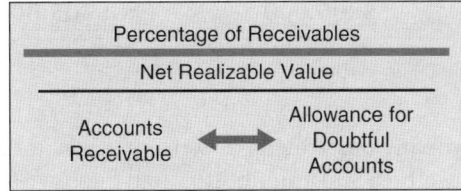
Balance Sheet Approach

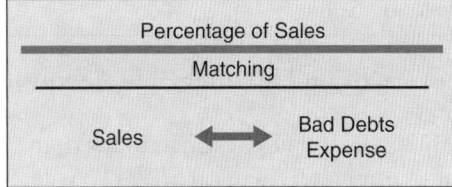
Income Statement Approach

Both the percentage of receivables and the percentage of sales approaches are generally accepted. The choice is a management decision.

The percentage of sales approach is quick and easy to use and it is aimed at achieving the most accurate matching of expenses to revenues.

The percentage of receivables approach is focused on presenting the correct net realizable value of accounts receivable in the balance sheet.

As accounting standards increasingly emphasize the balance sheet, it has been argued that the percentage of receivables approach is the most appropriate method to use.

2. Writing Off Uncollectible Accounts

Companies use various methods to collect past-due accounts. When all means of collecting appear impossible, the account should be written off. To prevent premature write offs, each write off should be approved in writing by management.

For example, Manahan Company authorizes the write off of a $300 balance owed by a customer, Ascott, on February 9, 2011. The journal entry to record the write off of this uncollectible account is as follows:

Feb. 9	Allowance for Doubtful Accounts	300	
	Accounts Receivable—Ascott		300
	To record write off of uncollectible account.		

> **TIP**
> **Bad Debts Expense is never used to record a write off** of an account. Bad debts expense is an estimate of uncollectible accounts for the current period, and is recorded at the end of the reporting period to ensure matching of expense to revenue. Remember that the bad debts expense account would be closed at the end of the period, during the closing process.

The write off affects only balance sheet accounts. The write off reduces both Accounts Receivable and the Allowance for Doubtful Accounts by the same amount, and so the net realizable value on the balance sheet remains the same. The effect of the above entry on the balance sheet accounts is shown on the following page:

	Before Write Off	After Write Off
Accounts Receivable	$ 230,000	$ 229,700
Less: Allowance for Doubtful Accounts	25,000	24,700
Net Realizable Value	**$205,000**	**$205,000**

3. Recovery of an Uncollectible Account

Sometimes a customer pays an amount that a company has previously written off as uncollectible. For example, on August 15, 2011, Ascott pays the $300 amount that had been written off on February 9. The entries to record the receipt from the customer are as follows:

Aug. 15	Accounts Receivable—Ascott	300	
	Allowance for Doubtful Accounts		300
	To reverse the write off of Ascott.		
Aug. 15	Cash	300	
	Accounts Receivable—Ascott		300
	To record collection from Ascott.		

When the entries are posted to the General Ledger control account, the customer's account in the subsidiary ledger must also be updated. This would update the customer's activity with the company and help when credit is being considered in the future.

Summary of Allowance Method

Three types of transactions may be used when valuing accounts receivable using the allowance method:
1. Estimates of uncollectible accounts receivable are recorded as adjusting entries at the end of the period by debiting Bad Debts Expense and crediting Allowance for Doubtful Accounts. The amount to record can be calculated using either the percentage of sales approach or the percentage of receivables approach.
2. Write offs of actual uncollectible accounts are recorded in the next accounting period by debiting Allowance for Doubtful Accounts and crediting Accounts Receivable.
3. Later recoveries, if any, are recorded in two separate entries. The first reverses the write off by debiting Accounts Receivable and crediting Allowance for Doubtful Accounts. The second records the normal collection of the account by debiting Cash and crediting Accounts Receivable.

These entries are summarized in the following T accounts:

Accounts Receivable			Allowance for Doubtful Accounts	
Beginning balance	Cash collections		Write offs	Beginning balance
Credit sales	Write offs			Later recoveries
Later recoveries				Bad debt adjusting entry
Ending balance				Ending balance

Notes Receivable

Study objective 3
Account for notes receivable.

Credit may also be granted in exchange for a formal credit instrument known as a **promissory note**. A promissory note is a written promise to pay a specified amount of money on demand or at a definite time. The party making the promise is called the maker; the party to whom the promise and eventual payment are made is called the payee. Credit may be granted in exchange for a promissory note.

The promissory note, identifying the payee by name or simply as the bearer, is a note receivable. The note details the names of the parties, the amount of the loan, the loan period, the interest rate, and the note due date, and gives the payee a legal claim to the borrower's assets.

A note receivable is a written promise to pay an amount owed, which gives the payee a legal claim. It differs from an account receivable, which is an informal promise to pay. The note is a negotiable instrument (similar to a cheque) and it can be transferred to another party when endorsed or signed by the payee.

The basic issues for notes receivable are similar to those of accounts receivable:
1. Recognizing notes receivable
2. Disposing of notes receivable

Recognizing Notes Receivable

A note receivable may be exchanged for an accounts receivable.

For example, the Alba Company accepts a $9,000 note receivable from Tross Ltd. in a settlement of an accounts receivable. The note has an interest rate of 5% per year and is due in six months on December 31. The entry to record the transaction is as follows:

July 1	Note Receivable—Tross Ltd.	9,000	
	Accounts Receivable—Tross Ltd.		9,000
	To record acceptance of the Tross note.		

When a note is exchanged for an account receivable, the customer might not have paid several invoices within a given 30-day period. The exchange, in settlement of this open account, would give the company a stronger legal claim to the funds owed by the customer.

Recording Interest

The interest rate specified on the note is always the rate of interest for one year (annual rate). Interest is calculated by applying the annual rate of interest to the note's face value, and then dividing the amount calculated by the number of months from date of issue to date of maturity.

The basic formula for calculating interest on an interest-bearing note is the following:

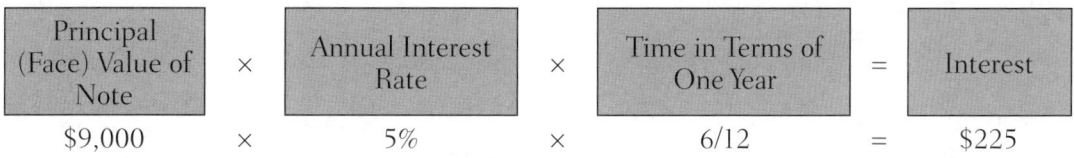

| Principal (Face) Value of Note | × | Annual Interest Rate | × | Time in Terms of One Year | = | Interest |
| $9,000 | × | 5% | × | 6/12 | = | $225 |

The Alba Company journal entry to record the interest owed for the month of July is as follows:

July 31	Interest Receivable	37.50	
	Interest Revenue ($9,000 × 5% × 1/12)		37.50
	To accrue interest on the Tross note receivable.		

Interest on the note receivable is recorded in a separate account. The note is a formal credit instrument and its recorded value stays at its face value.

Valuing Notes Receivable

Like accounts receivable, notes receivable are reported at their net realizable value. Each note must be analyzed to determine how likely it is to be collected, similar to accounts receivable. If eventual collection is doubtful, a bad debts expense and an allowance for doubtful notes must be recorded. Some companies use only one allowance account for both accounts and notes receivable. It is the Allowance for Doubtful Accounts.

Disposing of Notes Receivable

Notes receivable are held to their maturity when interest and any unpaid interest is due. This is known as honouring (paying) the note. If the maker of the note does not pay the amount owing at maturity, adjustments must be made to the accounts. This is known as dishonouring (not paying) the note.

Honouring of Notes Receivable

A note is honoured when it is paid in full at its maturity date. The amount due at maturity is the principal of the note plus interest for the length of time the note is outstanding (assuming interest is due at maturity).

For example, on July 1, the Alba Company accepts a $9,000 note receivable from Tross Ltd. in settlement of three accounts receivable. The note has an interest rate of 5% per year and is due in six months on December 31.

On December 31, the maturity date, Tross honoured the 6-month note by paying the face or principal amount, $9,000, plus interest of 5%. Assuming that interest has not been accrued, the entry made by Alba is as follows:

Dec. 31	Cash	9,225	
	Notes Receivable—Tross		9,000
	Interest Revenue		225
	To record collection of the Tross note.		

If the interest on the note had been accrued on a monthly basis, then at the end of each month from July through November, the accrual would have been identical to the one illustrated below for July:

July 31	Interest Receivable	37.50	
	Interest Revenue		37.50
	To record interest on the note for the month.		

At maturity of the note on December 31, the accrued interest would be $187.50 ($37.50 × 5) minus interest from July to November. The interest for December would now be earned. The Alba entry would be as follows:

Dec. 31	Cash	9,225.00	
	Notes Receivable—Tross		9,000.00
	Interest Receivable		187.50
	Interest Revenue		37.50
	To record collection of the Tross note with accrued interest.		

Dishonouring of Notes Receivable

A dishonoured note is a note that is not paid in full at maturity.

If, on December 31, Tross dishonoured or refused to pay the note, the following entry would be made (assuming interest had not been accrued on a monthly basis):

Dec. 31	Accounts Receivable—Tross	9,225	
	Notes Receivable		9,000
	Interest Revenue		225
	To record dishonouring of Tross note where collection is expected.		

If the amount owing is eventually collected, Alba will debit Cash and credit Accounts Receivable. If there were no hope of collection, the principal of the note would be written off by debiting the Allowance for Doubtful Accounts account and crediting the Notes Receivable account. No interest revenue would be recorded. If the interest were already accrued, the interest amount in the Interest Receivable would be debited.

Statement Presentation and Management of Receivables

Financial statement presentation of receivables is important because receivables are directly affected by how a company recognizes its revenue and bad debts expense. The reported numbers are also used when analyzing a company's liquidity and how well it manages its receivables.

Study objective 4
Demonstrate the presentation, analysis, and management of receivables.

Presentation

On the balance sheet, short-term receivables are reported within the current assets section following cash and short-term investments. Other receivables include interest receivable, loans or advances to employees, and recoverable sales and income taxes. These receivables are generally classified and reported as separate items in the current or non-current sections of the balance sheet, according to their due dates. Notes receivable may also be either current assets or long-term assets, depending on their due dates.

The net amount of receivables must be disclosed; however, it is helpful to report both the gross amount of receivables and the allowance for doubtful accounts either on the statement or in the notes to the financial statements. Notes receivable are often listed before accounts receivable because they are more easily converted to cash.

Analysis

The relationship between sales, accounts receivable, and cash collections is important in assessing the company's efficiency. A company's management of its receivables may be helping or hurting it. One way to assess this is to calculate a ratio called the receivables turnover ratio.

The **receivables turnover ratio** measures the number of times, on average, that receivables are collected during a period. The receivables turnover ratio is calculated as follows:

Net Credit Sales	÷	Average Gross Accounts Receivable	=	Receivables Turnover

A high ratio indicates that the company's receivables are more easily converted into cash. The average gross accounts receivable is calculated using the average of the opening and closing accounts receivable for the period. The receivables turnover is expressed in a figure representing the number of times that receivables are collected, on average.

A popular variation of the receivables turnover is to convert it into the number of days it takes the company to collect its receivables. This ratio, called the **collection period**, is used as a measure of the company's effectiveness in managing its credit sales and converting them to cash. It is calculated as follows:

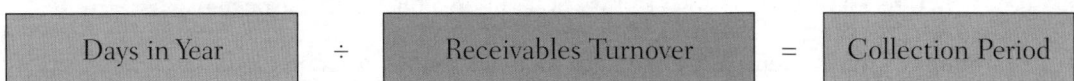

The collection period is expressed in days. It uses the 365 days in the year divided by the receivables turnover. The higher the receivables turnover, the fewer days it takes to convert the receivables to cash.

The collection period can also be used to assess the length of a company's operating cycle. Recall from Chapter 4 that the operating cycle is the average time that it takes to purchase inventory, sell it on account, and then collect cash from customers. In Chapter 6, we learned how to calculate days sales in inventory, which is the average age of the inventory on hand. The combination of the collection period and days sales in inventory is a useful way to measure the length of a company's operating cycle. The calculation is as follows:

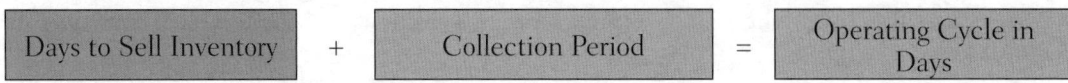

The ratio calculates the number of days, on average, it takes from the time a company purchases its inventory until it collects cash from sales.

Accelerating Cash Receipts from Receivables

As credit sales and receivables increase in size, waiting for receivables to be collected causes increased costs from not being able to immediately use the cash that will be collected. There are two ways to collect cash more quickly: using the receivables to secure a loan, and selling the receivables.

Loans Secured by Receivables
To speed up the cash flow, a company can borrow money from the bank using the accounts receivable as collateral. The company receives a loan, making cash available to it, and it pays interest on the bank loan. Banks may finance up to 75% of the receivables. Quite often the arrangement occurs through an operating line of credit.

Sale of Receivables
Receivables may be sold for cash to another company for the following reasons:
- The company's receivables are very large and it does not want to hold large amounts of receivables.
- The receivables are the only reasonable source of cash when the company's cash is low and the cost of borrowing may be too high.
- Billing and collection are often too time consuming and costly.

Factoring is a way to accelerate receivables collection by selling the receivables to a finance company or bank, known as a factor. The factor will buy the receivables from businesses and then collect the cash directly from the customer.

If the customer does not pay, the business is usually responsible for reimbursing the factor for the uncollected amounts. This is known as selling on a recourse basis.

Securitization of receivables is the process of transferring receivables to investors in return for cash. The receivables are sold to an independent trust, which holds the receivables as an investment. This transforms the receivables into securities of the trust. In some cases, the transfer is treated as a sale of receivables, or it may be treated as a secured loan.

The differences between factoring and securitization are that securitization involves many investors and the cost is lower, the receivables are of higher quality, and the seller usually continues to be involved with collecting the receivables. In factoring, the sale is usually to only one company, the cost is higher, the receivables quality is lower, and the seller does not normally have any involvement with collecting the receivables.

Demonstration Problem (SO 1, 2, & 3)

The December 31, 2010, balance sheet of Sparkle City Company reported the following amounts:

Accounts Receivable	$179,950
Allowance for Doubtful Accounts (credit)	4,200

The following transactions occurred during the following year:

Jan. 1 Accepted Barber Consultants' $10,000, 9-month, 12% note for the balance due on account. Interest is accrued every three months.

Feb. 5 Wrote off as uncollectible an account receivable from Stoldt Co. for $750 and an account receivable from Scanlon for $1,200.

Mar. 31 Interest on the note accepted from Barber Consultants was accrued to date.

May 26 Received $1,200 from Scanlon for the account receivable written off on February 5.

June 30 Interest on the note accepted from Barber Consultants was accrued from April 1 to date.

July 15 Received a 2-month, 6% note from Hammond to replace her account receivable balance of $5,000.

Sept. 15 Hammond dishonoured her note. It is expected that Hammond will still pay in the future.

Oct. 31 Barber Consultants honours its note receivable, and has sent the company a cheque in the amount owing plus interest to date.

Dec. 15 Hammond declared bankruptcy. Her account is written off as uncollectible.

Dec. 31 Using the percentage of receivables approach, Sparkle City estimates that 2% of accounts receivable will become uncollectible. Assume that no credit sales were recorded during 2011.

Instructions

a. Prepare the journal entries for Sparkle City's transactions.
b. Calculate the balance in the Allowance for Doubtful Accounts on December 31, 2011.

Solution to Demonstration Problem

a.

\multicolumn{3}{c}{General Journal}		J1
Date	Account Titles and Explanation	Debit	Credit
2011			
(a)			
Jan. 31	Notes Receivable—Barber	10,000	
	Accounts Receivable—Barber		10,000
	To record acceptance of Barber Consultants note.		
Feb. 5	Allowance for Doubtful Accounts	750	
	Accounts Receivable—Stoldt		750
	To write off account of Stoldt's accounts receivable.		
	Allowance for Doubtful Accounts	1,200	
	Accounts Receivable—Scanlon		1,200
	To write off account of Scanlon.		
Mar. 31	Interest Receivable—Barber	300	
	Interest Revenue		300
	To record interest accrued from January 1		
	to date ($10,000 × 12% × 3/12).		
May 26	Accounts Receivable—Scanlon	1,200	
	Allowance for Doubtful Accounts		1,200
	To reverse the Scanlon write off entry.		
	Cash	1,200	
	Accounts Receivable—Scanlon		1,200
	To record collection from Scanlon.		
June 30	Interest Receivable	300	
	Interest Revenue		300
	To record interest from April 1 to date.		
July 15	Notes Receivable	5,000	
	Accounts Receivable		5,000
	To receive a note to replace an account.		

Sept. 15	Accounts Receivable	5,050	
	Interest Revenue ($5,000 × 6% × 2/12)		50
	Notes Receivable		5,000
	To record Hammond's dishonoured note.		
Oct. 31	Cash	10,900	
	Interest Revenue		300
	Interest Receivable		600
	Notes Receivable		10,000
	To record Barber's note honoured.		
Dec. 15	Allowance for Doubtful Accounts	5,050	
	Accounts Receivable		5,050
	To record write off of Hammond's account.		
Dec. 31	Bad Debts Expense ($163,000 × 2%)*	3,260	
	Allowance for Doubtful Accounts		3,260
	To record estimated bad debts.		

* Accounts receivable ending balance = $179,950 − 10,000 − 750 − 1,200 + 1,200 − 1,200 − 5,000 + 5,050 − 5,050 = $163,000

b.

Balance, Jan. 1, 2010, Allowance for Doubtful Accounts			$4,200 Cr.
Receivable write off	Stoldt	$ 750	
Receivable write off	Scanlon	1,200	
Receivable reversal	Scanlon	(1,200)	
Receivable write off	Hammond	5,050	5,800 Dr.
Balance before allowance set up			1,600 Dr.
December 31 estimate of uncollectible accounts			3,260 Cr.
Balance, Dec. 31, 2011			$1,660 Cr.

Review Questions and Exercises

Multiple Choice

Circle the letter that best answers each of the following statements.

1. (SO 1) Which of the following items is not considered a receivable?
   a. Accounts receivable
   b. Nonbank credit cards
   c. Debit cards
   d. Trade receivables

2. (SO 1) On February 1, 2011, Lara Company sells merchandise on account to Livingston Company for $5,000. Lara Company uses the periodic inventory system. The entry to record this transaction by Lara Company is:

a. Sales   5,000
       Accounts Payable   5,000
b. Cash   5,000
       Sales   5,000
c. Accounts Receivable   5,000
       Sales   5,000
d. Notes Receivable   5,000
       Accounts Receivable   5,000

3. (SO 1) On March 1, 2011, Etheredge Company sells merchandise on account to Brooks Company for $7,000, terms n/30. Etheredge Company uses the periodic inventory system. On March 8, payment is received from Brooks for the balance due. The entry on March 8 by Etheredge is:

a. Sales   7,000
       Accounts Payable   7,000
b. Cash   7,000
       Sales   7,000
c. Cash   7,000
       Accounts Receivable   7,000
d. Notes Receivable   7,000
       Accounts Receivable   7,000

4. (SO 1) When an accounts receivable is recognized, it is posted to the general ledger, which acts as a control account, and also to:

   a. the Sales account, where the individual amount owing is recognized.
   b. the subsidiary ledger, where the individual accounts receivable is recognized.
   c. the merchandise inventory, as a debit to recognize the goods sold.
   d. the Sales account, to recognize the cost of the items sold.

5. (SO 1) When interest is charged to a customer's account, all of the following occur except:

   a. the customer's subsidiary accounts receivable increases.
   b. the seller recognizes an accrual of revenue.
   c. the account Interest Receivable is increased.
   d. the resulting effect is an increase in profit.

6. (SO 2) When the allowance method of recognizing bad debts expense is used, the entry to recognize that expense:

   a. increases profit.
   b. decreases current assets.
   c. has no effect on current assets.
   d. has no effect on profit.

7. (SO 2) An approach to estimating uncollectible accounts that focuses on the income statement rather than the balance sheet is the:
   a. direct write off of uncollectibles.
   b. aging of the accounts receivable.
   c. percentage of sales.
   d. percentage of receivables.

8. (SO 2) White Company estimates bad debts expense at 2% of credit sales. The following data are available for 2011:

Allowance for doubtful accounts, 1/1/2011	$ 21,000 (Cr.)
Accounts written off as uncollectible during 2011	13,000
Credit sales in 2011	3,000,000

   The Allowance for Doubtful Accounts balance at December 31, 2011, should be:
   a. $68,000.
   b. $60,000.
   c. $50,000.
   d. $13,000.

9. (SO 2) In 2011, the Rabindra Company had credit sales of $600,000 and granted sales allowances of $12,000. On January 1, 2011, Allowance for Doubtful Accounts had a credit balance of $15,000. During 2011, $25,000 of uncollectible accounts receivable were written off. Experience indicates that 3% of net credit sales become uncollectible. What should be the adjusted balance of Allowance for Doubtful Accounts at December 31, 2011?
   a. $7,640
   b. $8,000
   c. $17,640
   d. $33,000

10. (SO 2) An analysis and aging of the accounts receivable of Green Company at December 31 revealed the following data:

Accounts Receivable	$600,000
Allowance for Doubtful Accounts before adjustment	75,000 (Cr.)
Estimated uncollectible accounts	82,000

    The net realizable value of the accounts receivable at December 31, after adjustment, is:
    a. $583,000.
    b. $525,000.
    c. $518,000.
    d. $443,000.

11. (SO 2) Voight Company's account balances at December 31 for Accounts Receivable and Allowance for Doubtful Accounts were $1,400,000 and $70,000 (Cr.), respectively. An

aging of accounts receivable indicated that $108,000 is expected to become uncollectible. The amount of the adjusting entry for bad debts at December 31 is:

a. $108,000.
b. $38,000.
c. $178,000.
d. $70,000.

12. (SO 2) Bonnie Company decides that the past due account of Sheldon Stahl is uncollectible. Under the allowance method, the $865 balance owed by Sheldon Stahl is written off as follows:

a. Bad Debts Expense 865
    Accounts Receivable—S. Stahl 865
b. Allowance for Doubtful Accounts 865
    Accounts Receivable—S. Stahl 865
c. Accounts Receivable—S. Stahl 865
    Allowance for Doubtful Accounts 865
d. Allowance for Doubtful Accounts 865
    Bad Debts Expense 865

13. (SO 2) On October 18, the Aurora Company realizes that the $300 balance of Mary Vonesh that was written off as uncollectible is now collectible. The entry to restore the customer's account is:

a. Allowance for Doubtful Accounts 300
    Accounts Receivable—Mary Vonesh 300
b. Bad Debts Expense 300
    Allowance for Doubtful Accounts 300
c. Accounts Receivable—Mary Vonesh 300
    Allowance for Doubtful Accounts 300
d. Accounts Receivable—Mary Vonesh 300
    Bad Debts Expense 300

14. (SO 3) On February 1, Lowery Company received a $5,000, 9%, 4-month note receivable. Interest is due at maturity. The cash to be received by Lowery Company when the note becomes due is:

a. $150.
b. $5,000.
c. $5,150.
d. $5,450.

Questions 15 and 16 are based on the following information: On February 15, 2011, Gilbert Company received a 3-month, 9%, $2,000 note from Vincent Nathan for the settlement of his account receivable.

15. (SO 3) The entry by Gilbert Company on February 15, 2011 is:

a. Notes Receivable 2,000
    Accounts Receivable—V. Nathan 2,000

b. Accounts Receivable—V. Nathan   2,045
    Notes Receivable   2,045
c. Cash   2,045
    Interest Revenue   45
    Notes Receivable   2,000
d. Cash   2,000
    Accounts Receivable—V. Nathan   2,000

16. (SO 3) The entry by Gilbert Company on May 15, 2011, if Nathan dishonours the note and collection as expected is:

  a. Accounts Receivable—V. Nathan   2,045
      Notes Receivable   2,045
  b. Accounts Receivable—V. Nathan   2,045
      Notes Receivable   2,000
      Interest Revenue   45
  c. Accounts Receivable—V. Nathan   1,855
    Interest Lost   45
      Notes Receivable   2,000
  d. Bad Debts Expense   2,045
      Notes Receivable   2,045

17. (SO 3) All of the following are true except:
  a. An account receivable is an informal promise to pay an amount owing.
  b. An account receivable is the same as a note receivable.
  c. A note receivable is a written promise to pay an amount owing.
  d. A note receivable can be transferred to another party by endorsement.

18. (SO 3) A note receivable could have which of the following characteristics:
  a. It bears interest for the period of the note.
  b. It could result from a purchase or a loan.
  c. It could result from extending an account receivable beyond normal amounts or due dates.
  d. It could be a result of all or any of the above.

19. (SO 3) Which one of the following statements about notes receivable and accounts receivable is correct?
  a. They are both interest bearing for the period that they exist.
  b. They are both credit instruments.
  c. They are both valued at their net realizable values.
  d. They can be sold to another party.

20. (SO 4) In the financial statement presentation of receivables:
  a. it is not necessary to identify the major types of receivables.
  b. only the gross amount of receivables must be disclosed.
  c. bad debts are reported as an operating expense on the income statement.
  d. accounts receivable are always listed before notes receivable because accounts receivable are more important.

21. (SO 4) A company may sell its receivables for any of the following reasons except:
    a. it needs cash and may not be able to borrow money in the credit market.
    b. it does not want to hold a large amount of receivables.
    c. the billing and collection of receivables are costly and time consuming.
    d. billing and collection are not acceptable and it is converting to a cash-only system.

22. (SO 3, 4) Which of the following statements concerning receivables is incorrect?
    a. Notes receivable are often listed under long-term assets.
    b. Notes receivable give the maker a stronger legal claim to assets than accounts receivable.
    c. Both the gross amount of receivables and the allowance for doubtful accounts should be reported.
    d. Interest revenue and gain on sale of notes receivable are shown under other revenues and gains.

Matching

Match each term with its definition by writing the appropriate letter in the space provided.

Terms

____ 1. Promissory note

____ 2. Aging of accounts receivable

____ 3. Percentage of sales approach

____ 4. Allowance method

____ 5. Percentage of receivables approach

____ 6. Net realizable value

____ 7. Dishonoured note

____ 8. Honoured note

____ 9. Maker

____ 10. Payee

Definitions

a. An approach to estimating uncollectible accounts where bad debts expense is calculated as a percentage of credit sales.

b. The net amount of receivables expected to be received in cash.

c. A method of accounting for bad debts that is required when bad debts are material.

d. The party that promises to pay a promissory note.

e. A note that is not paid in full at maturity.

f. A written promise to pay a specified amount of money on demand or at a definite time.

g. An approach to estimating uncollectible accounts where the allowance for doubtful accounts is calculated as a percentage of receivables.

h. An analysis of individual customer accounts by the length of time they have been unpaid.

i. The party to whom a promissory note is to be paid.

j. A note that is paid in full at maturity.

Exercises

E8—1 (SO 2) The L. Riel Co. had a credit balance in Allowance for Doubtful Accounts of $10,000 at January 1, 2011. During 2011, credit sales totalled $300,000. A summary of the aging of accounts receivable at December 31, 2011, is as follows:

Classification by Month of Sale	Balance in Each Category	Estimated % Uncollectible
Nov. – Dec. 2011	$ 60,000	2%
Jul. – Oct. 2011	30,000	10
Jan. – June 2011	10,000	25
Prior to 1/1/2011	5,000	75
	$105,000	

On April 2, 2011, $750 was received from Tom Scott; his account for $750 had been written off as uncollectible in 2009. During 2011, accounts receivable totalling $8,400 were written off as uncollectible.

Instructions
a. Record the April 2 collection of the account previously written off.

b. Prepare a summary entry for the accounts written off in 2011 dated Dec. 31.

c. Assuming L. Riel Co. estimates uncollectibles as 2% of credit sales, prepare the December 31, 2011, adjusting entry.

d. Instead assume that L. Riel Co. estimates uncollectibles by using the percentage of accounts receivable. Prepare the December 31, 2011, adjusting entry (use the aging schedule if necessary).

	General Journal		J1
Date	**Account Titles and Explanation**	**Debit**	**Credit**
2011			
(a)			
(b)			

(c)

(d)

E8—2 (SO 3) Burton Company had the following transactions for the year ended December 31, 2011:

July	1	Received a $2,000, 3-month, 8% promissory note from Richard Newman in settlement of an open account. Interest is payable at maturity.
Aug.	1	Received a $1,000, 3-month, 10% note receivable from Suzanne Hurley for cash borrowed by Hurley. Interest is payable at maturity.
Oct.	1	Received notice that the Richard Newman note had been dishonoured. It is expected that Newman will eventually pay the amount owed.
Nov.	1	Hurley honoured the note receivable in full. (Assume that interest has not been accrued.)

Instructions
Prepare the entries for the transactions above.

General Journal			J1
Date	Account Titles and Explanation	Debit	Credit
2011			

E8—3 (SO 3) The Bego Company adjusts its books monthly. On June 30, 2011, selected ledger account balances are as follows:

        Notes Receivable $44,200
        Interest Receivable   315

Notes Receivable include the following:

Date	Maker	Principal	Interest	Term
Apr. 1	Karam Inc.	$10,000	7%	6 months
May 1	Lyttle Co.	9,000	5%	3 months
June 1	Meyer Inc.	6,000	10%	6 months
June 15	Sulit Ltd.	7,200	5%	4 months
June 30	Rinas Corp.	12,000	9%	6 months

Instructions
a. Prepare a schedule calculating the Interest Receivable at June 30.
b. Prepare the entry to record the full payment of the Karam note at maturity on September 30, 2011 (round answers to the nearest dollar).

a. _____

b. _____

E8—4 (SO 1 & 3)

1. On May 1, 2011, the Shaloy Company sold merchandise to E. Dale. She used her Shaloy credit card, which has an interest charge of 20% per annum. On the payment date on her statement, June 3, she was not able to pay the balance of her account, $3,000, and was charged a financing charge for the first month she was overdue.
2. Everson Retailers, a customer of the Shaloy Company, signed a promissory note that was due on June 1. Shaloy accepted the note, in the amount of $10,000 at 6% for three months, when three invoices from Everson remained unpaid. Interest is to be accrued monthly.

Instructions

a. Record Shaloy's entry on June 3 to record the interest charged to E. Dale.
b. Record Shaloy's entry to record accepting the note receivable from Everson.
c. Record the interest accrued on the Everson note at the end of the first month.
d. Why is the interest on the overdue accounts receivable added to the customer account, but the interest on the note receivable is recorded separately?

a. _____

b. _____

c. _____

d. _____

E8—5 (SO 4) The following information was taken from the records of the Minimoore Company:

Accounts Receivable December 31, 2011	$ 235,000
Accounts Receivable December 31, 2010	$ 189,000
Sales	$1,535,000

Sales Returns and Allowances	$ 35,000
Allowance for Doubtful Accounts 2010	$ 28,000
Allowance for Doubtful Accounts 2011	$ 30,000

Instructions
a. Calculate (1) the receivables turnover and (2) the collection period.
b. If the receivables turnover for the previous year was 20 times and the collection period was 18.25 days, comment on the company's performance over the two years.

a. _____

b. _____

Solutions to Review Questions and Exercises

Multiple Choice

1. (c) Debit cards are considered cash. Accounts receivable, also called trade receivables, (a) and (d), are amounts owed by customers on account. Nonbank credit cards (b) are considered receivables.

2. (c) When a business sells merchandise on credit, in addition to the revenue earned and recorded as Sales, it must recognize the increase to Accounts Receivable by debiting the asset account.

3. (c) The correct entry is Cash (Dr.) $7,000 and Accounts Receivable (Cr.) $7,000.

4. (b) Receivables are posted to the Accounts Receivable—a control account—and also to the Subsidiary Accounts Receivable ledger, where individual customer accounts are kept.

5. (c) Items (a), (b), and (d) are all true. The exception is item (c), where interest is not debited to Interest Receivable. It is debited to the Accounts Receivable account and to the customer's subsidiary account to recognize the additional interest amount owing.

6. (b) Estimated uncollectibles are debited to Bad Debts Expense and credited to Allowance for Doubtful Accounts. The Allowance for Doubtful Accounts is a contra asset account to Accounts Receivable. When it is offset against Accounts Receivable, it decreases the current assets to its net realizable value.

7. (c) The allowance method using the percentage of sales approach focuses on the income statement. The aging of the accounts receivable (b) and a percentage of the accounts receivable (d) focus on the balance sheet.

8. (a) The balance in the Allowance for Doubtful Accounts prior to adjustment is a credit of $8,000 ($21,000 − $13,000). The adjusting entry under the percentage of sales method is $60,000 ($3,000,000 × 2%). Thus, the adjusted balance is $68,000 ($8,000 + $60,000).

9. (a) The balance in Allowance for Doubtful Accounts prior to adjustment is a debit of $10,000 ($25,000 − $15,000). The adjusting entry is $17,640 [($600,000 − $12,000) × 3%]. Thus the new balance is $7,640 ($17,640 − $10,000).

10. (c) The net realizable value of the accounts receivable at December 31 should be accounts receivable ($600,000) less the new balance of the allowance for doubtful accounts ($82,000), or $518,000.

11. (b) Under the percentage of receivables approach, the allowance account is adjusted to the estimated uncollectibles. In this case, the required balance is $108,000 and the amount of the adjusting entry is $38,000 ($108,000 − $70,000).

12. (b) Under the allowance method, every bad debt write off is made against the allowance account. The write off of the account reduces both Accounts Receivable and Allowance for Doubtful Accounts. A debit to Bad Debts Expense is used only when the adjusting entry is made for estimated bad debts.

13. (c) When an uncollectible account already written off becomes collectible, the entry to restore the customer account is a debit to Accounts Receivable and a credit to the Allowance for Doubtful Accounts.

14. (c) When a Note Receivable becomes due, interest together with the principal amount is due to the maker of the note. Interest calculated ($5,000 × 9% × 4/12 = $150) is added to the principal of $5,000. Total cash received is $5,150.

15. (a) A transfer from one asset account, Accounts Receivable, to another asset account, Notes Receivable, is made by debiting Notes Receivable and crediting Accounts Receivable.

16. (b) If the note is dishonoured, the Notes Receivable reverts to Accounts Receivable. The amount of interest that has been earned, $45 ($2,000 × 9% × 3/12), is recognized by crediting Interest Revenue and by increasing Accounts Receivable.

17. (b) An account receivable is different from a note receivable. A note gives the payee a stronger legal claim to the amount owing.

18. (d) Items (a), (b), and (c) are all characteristics of notes receivable.

19. (a) Accounts receivable do not incur interest unless the account is overdue. Notes receivable usually bear interest for the entire period.

20. (c) Bad debts expense is included in operating expenses because bad debts are the result of an operating decision—the decision to sell on credit.

21. (d) Most companies extend credit to attract customers. Changing to a cash-only system is not good for business, nor is it a reason to sell the receivables. Items (a), (b), and (c) are the reasons receivables are sold.

22. (a) Notes receivable are listed in current assets. Answers (b), (c), and (d) are all correct.

Matching

1. f
2. h
3. a
4. c
5. g
6. b
7. e
8. j
9. d
10. i

Exercises

E8—1

	General Journal		J1
Date	Account Titles and Explanation	Debit	Credit
2011			
a.			
April 2	Accounts Receivable—T. Scott	750	
	Allowance for Doubtful Accounts		750
	To reverse write off of T. Scott account.		
April 2	Cash	750	
	Accounts Receivable—T. Scott		750
	To record collection from T. Scott.		

b.

Dec. 31	Allowance for Doubtful Accounts	8,400	
	Accounts Receivable		8,400
	To write off 2008 uncollectible accounts.		

c.

Dec. 31	Bad Debts Expense ($300,000 × 2%)	6,000	
	Allowance for Doubtful Accounts		6,000
	To record estimated bad debts for year.		

d.

Dec. 31	Bad Debts Expense	8,100	
	Allowance for Doubtful Accounts		8,100*
	To adjust allowance account to total estimated uncollectibles.		

d. (continued)

Aging Schedule

Classification by Month of Sale	Balance in Each Category	Estimated % Uncollectible	Estimated Bad Debts
Nov. – Dec. 2011	$ 60,000	2%	$ 1,200
July – Oct. 2011	30,000	10	3,000
Jan. – June 2011	10,000	25	2,500
Prior to 1/1/2011	5,000	75	3,750
	$105,000		$10,450

* The balance in Allowance for Doubtful Accounts prior to adjustment is $2,350 (Cr.) ($10,000 + $750 – $8,400). Therefore, the adjusting entry is $8,100 ($10,450 – $2,350).

E8—2

General Journal			J1
Date	Account Titles and Explanation	Debit	Credit
2011			
July 1	Notes Receivable	2,000	
	Accounts Receivable—R. Newman		2,000
	To record acceptance of R. Newman note.		
Aug. 1	Notes Receivable	1,000	
	Cash		1,000
	To record acceptance of S. Hurley note.		

Oct. 1	Accounts Receivable	2,040	
	Notes Receivable		2,000
	Interest Revenue ($2,000 × 8% × 3/12)		40
	To record dishonouring of the R. Newman		
	note; expect to collect in the future.		
Nov. 1	Cash	1,025	
	Notes Receivable		1,000
	Interest Revenue ($1,000 × 10% × 3/12)		25
	To record honouring of S. Hurley note.		

E8—3

a.

Karam Inc $10,000 × 7% × 3/12	=	$175.00	
Lyttle Co. $ 9,000 × 5% × 2/12	=	75.00	
Meyer Inc. $ 6,000 × 10% × 1/12	=	50.00	
Sulit Ltd. $ 7,200 × 5% × 0.5/12	=	15.00	
		$315.00	

b. 2011

Sept. 30	Cash	10,350	
	Notes Receivable		10,000
	Interest Receivable (5 months accrued)		292
	Interest Revenue		58
	To record payment of note at maturity.		

E8—4

a. June 3 Accounts Receivable—Dale   50
           Interest Revenue   50
           To record service fees on overdue account.

b. June 1 Notes Receivable   10,000
           Accounts Receivable   10,000
           To record acceptance of Everson's note.

c. June 30 Interest Receivable   50
           Interest Revenue   50
           To record interest accrued on note.

d. Though both accounts receivable and notes receivable are interest bearing, interest charges are added to the balance due if a customer does not pay the account in full within a specified period (usually 30 days). The interest on the notes payable becomes due at the maturity of the notes payable, as the legal claim states, and is not due until the note's maturity date. Also, the note receivable remains at its historical cost.

E8—5

a. (1) Receivables turnover = $1,500,000 ÷ ([235,000 + 189,000] ÷ 2)
= $1,500,000 ÷ $212,000
= 7 times

(2) Collection period = 365 ÷ 7
= 52 days

b. The receivables turnover measures the company's efficiency in converting its credit sales into cash. The collection period is used to assess the effectiveness of the credit and collection policy. The receivables turnover has dropped from 20 times to 7 times. That means that the company efficiency in converting credit sales to cash has decreased. The collection period has increased from 18.25 days to 52 days. The company has not collected as efficiently in this period and should reconsider its credit and collection policies.

chapter | 9

chapter 9
Long-Lived Assets

Study objectives >>

After studying this chapter, you should be able to:
1. Determine the cost of property, plant, and equipment.
2. Explain and calculate depreciation.
3. Explain the factors that cause changes in periodic depreciation and calculate revisions.
4. Account for the disposal of property, plant, and equipment.
5. Calculate and record depreciation of natural resources.
6. Identify the basic accounting issues for intangible assets and goodwill.
7. Illustrate the reporting and analysis of long-lived assets.

Preview of Chapter 9

In this chapter, we explain how to determine the cost of long-lived assets such as property, plant, and equipment; natural resources; and intangible assets and goodwill. We also describe the methods used to allocate an asset's cost over its useful life. In addition, we discuss the accounting for expenditures incurred during the useful life of assets and the disposition of the assets at the end of their useful lives. The chapter is organized as follows:

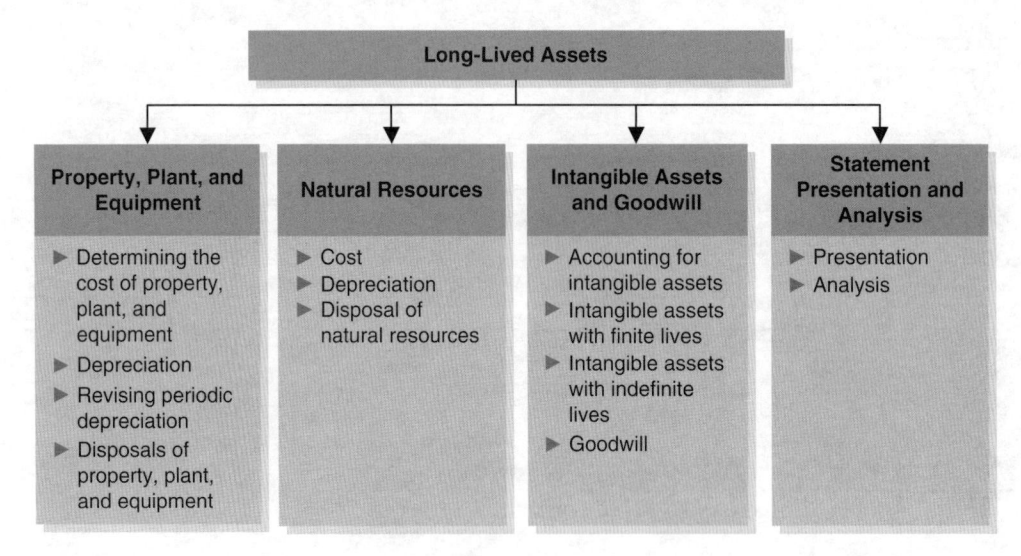

Long-Lived Assets

- **Property, Plant, and Equipment**
  - Determining the cost of property, plant, and equipment
  - Depreciation
  - Revising periodic depreciation
  - Disposals of property, plant, and equipment
- **Natural Resources**
  - Cost
  - Depreciation
  - Disposal of natural resources
- **Intangible Assets and Goodwill**
  - Accounting for intangible assets
  - Intangible assets with finite lives
  - Intangible assets with indefinite lives
  - Goodwill
- **Statement Presentation and Analysis**
  - Presentation
  - Analysis

Property, Plant, and Equipment

Property, plant, and equipment (also commonly known as fixed assets; land, building, and equipment; or capital assets) are long-lived assets that are used for the production and sale of goods and/or services to consumers. They have three characteristics:
1. They have a physical substance (a definite size and shape).
2. They are used in the operations of the business.
3. They are not intended for sale to customers.

Determining the Cost of Property, Plant, and Equipment

Study objective 1
Determine the cost of property, plant, and equipment.

Property, plant, and equipment are recorded at cost. Cost includes all expenditures made to acquire the asset (the purchase price, plus any non-refundable taxes, less any discounts or rebates) and expenditures necessary to bring the asset to the location and to the condition necessary to make it ready for its intended use.

Costs that are capitalized rather than expensed will provide benefits over future periods. These costs are called **capital expenditures**. Costs that benefit future periods are included in a long-lived asset account.

For example, if you buy land with an old building on it and you intend to erect a new building, the cost of wrecking the old building becomes a cost of the land. The wrecking costs are capital expenditures, not expensed.

Costs that benefit only the current period are expensed and are called **operating expenditures**.

Once the cost of an asset is established, it becomes the basis of accounting for the asset over its useful life. Even if or when an asset increases in value, the current fair value is not used after the asset is acquired. Cost is only adjusted if there is a permanent decline of the asset below the carrying amount.

Property, plant, and equipment are often subdivided into four classes:
1. Land, such as a building site
2. Land improvements, such as driveways, parking lots, fences, and underground sprinkler systems
3. Buildings, such as stores, offices, factories, and warehouses
4. Equipment, such as store checkout counters, cash registers, coolers, office furniture, factory machinery, and delivery equipment

1. Land
The cost of land includes (1) the purchase price; (2) closing costs such as surveying and legal fees; and (3) the costs of preparing the land for its intended use such as the removal of old buildings, clearing, draining, filling, and grading. All these costs become part of the total cost of the land (less any proceeds from salvaged materials) and would be debited to the Land account, with the credit going to whichever account explains the means of purchase, such as Cash or Mortgage Payable. Land is a long-lived asset; its cost is not depreciated because land has an unlimited useful life.

2. Land Improvements
Land improvements are structural additions made to the land. Land improvements such as driveways, sidewalks, fences, parking lots, and landscaping require maintenance and replacement to retain their value. They have limited useful lives and are depreciated over their useful lives. These costs are recorded separately from the cost of land.

3. Buildings
The costs debited to the Buildings account include all costs related to the purchase or construction of a building. Costs include the purchase price, closing costs (such as legal fees), and costs to make the building ready for its intended use, such as remodelling, and for replacing or repairing the roof, floors, wiring, and plumbing.

When a new building is constructed, costs consist of the contract price plus payments made for architects' fees, building permits, and excavation costs. Interest payments on funds borrowed for the construction are included in the asset cost when there is a considerable amount of time needed to get the building ready for use. Once the building is ready for use, further interest payments are debited to Interest Expense.

4. Equipment
Equipment includes delivery equipment, office equipment, machinery, vehicles, furniture and fixtures, and other similar assets. The cost of equipment consists of the purchase price and other related costs, such as freight charges and insurance during transit, paid by the purchaser. Other included costs are all expenditures required to assemble, install, and test the unit. These costs are capital expenditures.

All capital expenditures benefit future periods. Annual recurring costs such as licences and insurance are not capital expenditures because they do not benefit future periods.

Multiple Assets

Property, plant, and equipment are often purchased together for a single price. This is known as a **basket purchase** (or lump sum purchase). The total price paid for the group of property, plant, and equipment must be allocated to each individual asset in order to later calculate the depreciation of each individual asset. When a basket purchase occurs, we determine individual costs by allocating the total price paid for the group of assets to each individual asset based on its relative fair value.

Significant Components

When an item of property, plant, and equipment includes components with costs that are significant relative to its total cost, the cost of the item must be allocated to its different components. This is necessary so that each component can be separately depreciated over the different useful lives or possibly by using different depreciation methods.

Separating the cost of the entire asset into its significant components can be accomplished using the same process to allocate cost illustrated above for a basket purchase. The asset's total cost would be allocated to the significant components based on the components' relative fair values.

Component accounting is a new requirement for Canadian companies, resulting from the change to International Financial Reporting Standards (IFRS). Implementing it will likely require more detailed accounting records than many Canadian companies may have maintained under Canadian accounting standards. For simplicity, we will assume in this study guide that all of the components of the depreciable asset have the same useful life, and we will depreciate assets as a whole.

Depreciation

Study objective 2
Explain and calculate depreciation.

Under IFRS, companies have two models they can choose between to account for their property, plant, and equipment: the cost model or the revaluation model.

The cost model records property, plant, and equipment at cost of acquisition. After acquisition, depreciation is recorded each period and the assets are carried at cost less accumulated depreciation.

Under the revaluation model, the carrying amount of property, plant, and equipment is its fair value less any subsequent accumulated depreciation less any subsequent impairment losses. This model can be applied only to assets whose fair value can be reliably measured, and revaluations must be carried out often enough that the carrying amount is not materially different from the asset's fair value at the balance sheet date. As the accounting in the revaluation model is relatively complex, and because so few companies will use this model, we will not cover this model in this study guide.

Depreciation is the allocation of the cost of a long-lived asset to expense over its useful life. Depreciation is a cost allocation. It is not the accumulation of cash for the replacement of the asset or a process of determining an asset's real value. Rather it is the allocation of the cost of using up the asset over its useful life. During a depreciable asset's useful life, its revenue-producing ability declines because of physical factors such as wear and tear, and economic factors such as obsolescence.

When the adjustment for depreciation is recorded, the entry debits Depreciation Expense and credits Accumulated Depreciation. The Accumulated Depreciation account is a contra account to its related depreciable asset account. Thus, the asset account (Dr.), less its contra account, Accumulated Depreciation (Cr.), gives the asset's carrying amount.

Land improvements, buildings, and equipment are depreciable assets because their usefulness to the company and their revenue-producing ability decrease during their useful lives. Land is not depreciated because its life is unlimited and its ability to produce revenue is generally the same over time.

Depreciation is only an estimate of the asset's decline in value. Sometimes a decline in an asset's revenue-producing ability may occur because of obsolescence. For example, a company may replace its computers long before they wear out because of hardware and software improvements.

Factors in Calculating Depreciation
Three factors affect the calculation of depreciation:
1. **Cost** includes all costs incurred to obtain the asset and make it ready for its intended use.
2. **Useful life** is an estimate of (a) the period of time over which an asset is expected to be available for use, or (b) the number of units of production (such as machine hours) or units of output that are expected to be obtained from an asset.
3. **Residual value** is the estimated amount that a company would currently obtain from disposing of the asset if the asset were already at the end of its useful life and in the condition it is expected to be at the end of its useful life.

Depreciation Methods
Depreciation is generally calculated using one of three methods:
1. Straight-line
2. Diminishing-balance (sometimes called the declining-balance method)
3. Units-of-production (sometimes called the units-of-activity method)

Management must choose the method that best matches the estimated pattern in which the asset's future economic benefits are expected to be consumed. The depreciation method must be reviewed at least once a year. If the expected pattern of consumption of the future economic benefits has changed, the depreciation method must be changed. The estimated useful life and residual values must also be reviewed each year.

Straight-Line. Under the straight-line method, depreciation is the same for each year of the asset's useful life.

The formula for calculating annual depreciation expense is the following:

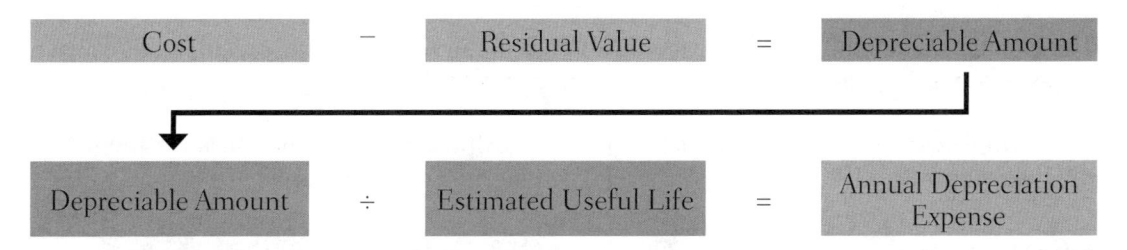

Cost − Residual Value = Depreciable Amount

Depreciable Amount ÷ Estimated Useful Life = Annual Depreciation Expense

For example, assume that the Benson Company purchased a delivery truck for $31,000 on January 1, with an estimated residual value of $2,000 at the end of its four-year useful life. The calculation of annual depreciation would be as follows:

($31,000 − $2,000) = $29,000

($29,000 ÷ 4) = $7,250

Alternatively, straight-line depreciation can be calculated by dividing 100% by the estimated useful life of the asset and applying that rate to the depreciable amount.

Using the example above:

(100% ÷ 4 years) × ($31,000 − $2,000) = depreciation expense

25% × $29,000 = $7,250

Year	Depreciable Amount		Depreciation Rate		Annual Depreciation Expense	End of Year Accumulated Depreciation	End of Year Carrying Amount
							$31,000
1	$29,000	×	25%	=	$ 7,250	$ 7,250	23,750
2	29,000	×	25%	=	7,250	14,500	16,500
3	29,000	×	25%	=	7,250	21,750	9,250
4	29,000	×	25%	=	7,250	29,000	2,000
					$29,000		

When the asset is purchased during the year, depreciation expense is pro-rated for the time the asset was used. Calculation should be rounded to the nearest month since depreciation is an estimate.

The straight-line method of depreciation is simple to apply. Under IFRS, the depreciation method used must be consistent with the pattern in which the economic benefits from owning the asset are expected to be consumed. Therefore, it is appropriate to use the straight-line method when the asset is used quite uniformly throughout its useful life.

Diminishing-Balance. The diminishing-balance method produces a decreasing annual depreciation expense over the asset's useful life. Unlike other depreciation methods, the diminishing-balance method does not use a depreciable amount. The depreciation rate remains constant from year to year, but the rate is applied to a carrying amount that declines each year. Annual depreciation expense is calculated by multiplying the carrying amount at the beginning of the year by the depreciation rate.

The residual value limits the total depreciation that can be taken. Depreciation stops when the asset's carrying amount equals its expected residual value.

The formula for calculating depreciation expense using the diminishing-balance method is the following:

Carrying Amount at Beginning of Year	×	Depreciation Rate	=	Annual Depreciation Expense

For example, the Benson Company uses a diminishing-balance rate of 40% to depreciate an asset that cost $31,000. The estimated residual value is $2,000. Depreciation is calculated as follows:

Year	Carrying Amount Beginning of Year		Depreciation Rate		Annual Depreciation Expense	End of Year Accumulated Depreciation	End of Year Carrying Amount
							$31,000
1	$31,000	×	40%	=	$12,400	$12,400	18,600
2	18,600	×	40%	=	7,440	19,840	11,160
3	11,160	×	40%	=	4,464	24,304	6,696
4	6,696	×	40%	=	4,696*	29,000	2,000
					$29,000		

*The depreciation expense for year 4, calculated using the depreciation rate, is $2,678 (rounded to the nearest dollar). However, this is the end of the asset's useful life so depreciation is calculated so that the carrying amount equals its estimated residual value ($29,000 residual value − $12,400 − $7,440 − $4,464 = $4,696). The residual value is accounted for at the end of the depreciation process, rather than at the beginning.

Varying rates of depreciation may be used, depending on how fast the company wants to depreciate the asset. You will find rates such as one time (single), two times (double), and even three times (triple) the straight-line rate of depreciation. A depreciation rate that is often used is double the straight-line rate. This method is referred to as the double diminishing-balance method.

The following example shows Benson Company using the double diminishing-balance depreciation method to calculate the depreciation of an asset costing $31,000 with an estimated residual value of $2,000. The rate is calculated as follows:
100% ÷ 4 = 25% × 2 = 50%

Year	Carrying Amount Beginning of Year		Double Diminishing-Balance Depreciation Rate		Annual Depreciation Expense	End of Year Accumulated Depreciation	End of Year Carrying Amount
							$31,000
1	$31,000	×	50%	=	$15,500	$15,500	15,500
2	15,500	×	50%	=	7,750	23,250	7,750
3	7,750	×	50%	=	3,875	27,125	3,875
4	3,875	×	50%	=	1,875*	29,000	2,000
					$29,000		

*The depreciation expense for year 4, calculated using the 50% depreciation rate, is $1,938 (rounded to the nearest dollar). However, this is the end of the asset's useful life so depreciation is calculated so that the carrying amount equals its estimated residual value ($29,000 residual value – $15,500 – $7,750 – $3,875 = $1,875). The residual value is accounted for at the end of the depreciation process, rather than at the beginning.

Under the diminishing-balance method, the depreciation rate remains constant from year to year, but the carrying amount to which the rate is applied declines each year. The diminishing-balance method is considered an accelerated depreciation method.

Units-of-Production. Under the units-of-production method, useful life is either the estimated total units of production or total expected use from the asset.

For example, the Benson Company has a truck purchased for $31,000 and expects to drive the truck for 200,000 kilometres. The estimated residual value is $2,000. In the first year, the truck is driven 30,000 kilometres. The formula for calculating depreciation expense is the following:

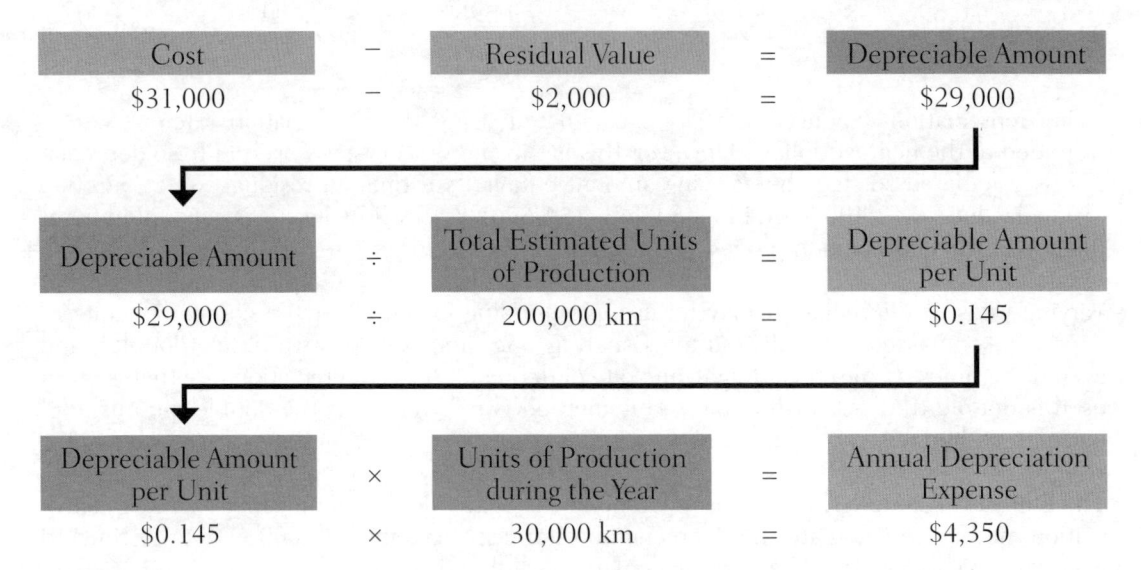

$$\text{Cost} - \text{Residual Value} = \text{Depreciable Amount}$$
$$\$31,000 - \$2,000 = \$29,000$$

$$\text{Depreciable Amount} \div \text{Total Estimated Units of Production} = \text{Depreciable Amount per Unit}$$
$$\$29,000 \div 200,000 \text{ km} = \$0.145$$

$$\text{Depreciable Amount per Unit} \times \text{Units of Production during the Year} = \text{Annual Depreciation Expense}$$
$$\$0.145 \times 30,000 \text{ km} = \$4,350$$

Assuming that the kilometres driven in year 2 are 60,000, year 3 are 50,000, and year 4 are 60,000 the depreciation schedule is completed as follows:

Year	Units of Production		Depreciable Amount/Unit		Depreciation Expense	End of Year Accumulated Depreciation	End of Year Carrying Amount
							$31,000
1	30,000	×	$0.145	=	$ 4,350	$ 4,350	26,650
2	60,000	×	$0.145	=	8,700	13,050	17,950
3	50,000	×	$0.145	=	7,250	20,300	10,700
4	60,000	×	$0.145	=	8,700	29,000	2,000
	200,000			=	$29,000		

In using this units-of-production method, it is often difficult to make a reasonable estimate of total production. When an asset's productive capacity varies significantly from one period to another, this method results in the best matching of expenses with revenues. In real life, when the total actual units of production does not exactly equal the total estimated units of production, the final year's depreciation is usually adjusted so that the ending carrying amount is equal to the estimated residual value.

When the asset is purchased during the year, depreciation expense is not pro-rated for the time the asset was used, because the units-of-production method is based on actual units produced during the period rather than how long the asset was used during the period.

Comparison of Depreciation Methods

If we assume for simplicity, that profit for Benson Company before deducting depreciation expense is $50,000 for each of the four years, with other expenses being constant, the impact of the differing depreciation methods can be compared as follows:

Year	Straight-Line Depreciation Expense	Profit	Double Diminishing-Balance Depreciation Expense	Profit	Units-of-Production Depreciation Expense	Profit
1	$ 7,250	$ 42,750	$15,500	$ 34,500	$ 4,350	$ 45,650
2	7,250	42,750	7,750	42,250	8,700	41,300
3	7,250	42,750	3,875	46,125	7,250	42,750
4	7,250	42,750	1,875	48,125	8,700	41,300
	$29,000	$171,000	$29,000	$171,000	$29,000	$171,000

Straight-line gives a constant amount of depreciation expense and profit in each year. Diminishing-balance results in a higher depreciation expense in early years and thus lower income, but lower depreciation expense in later years and thus higher income. The units-of-production method varies since depreciation expense depends on the actual usage of the asset each year.

Companies should choose the method that best matches the estimated pattern in which the asset's economic benefits are expected to be consumed. If the economic benefit of owning an asset is fairly consistent over time, the straight-line method is appropriate. The diminishing-balance method is appropriate if the company receives more economic benefit in the early years of the asset's useful life than in the later years. The units-of-production method is appropriate for assets whose usage varies over time. Because companies have more than one type of asset, they often use more than one depreciation method.

Depreciation and Income Tax

The Canada Revenue Agency (CRA) allows taxpayers to deduct depreciation expense when calculating taxable income. For accounting purposes, a company must choose the depreciation method that best reflects the pattern in which the asset's future economic benefits are consumed.

Depreciation, allowed for income tax purposes, is calculated on a group basis and is called **capital cost allowance (CCA)**.

The CRA does not permit taxpayers to estimate the useful life or depreciation rates of assets. It groups assets into various classes and provides maximum depreciation rates for each class. It also sets the rules for partial depreciation for assets purchased during a current year. CRA requires taxpayers to use the single diminishing-balance method on the tax return, regardless of what method is used in the financial statement to calculate depreciation expense.

Revising Periodic Depreciation

Study objective 3
Explain the factors that cause changes in periodic depreciation and calculate revisions.

Depreciation needs to be revised if there are changes in any of the three factors that affect depreciation: the asset's cost, useful life, and residual value. Revisions are made if there are any of the following changes:
1. Capital expenditures made during the asset's useful life
2. Impairments in the asset's fair value
3. Changes in the asset's fair value when using the revaluation model
4. Changes in the appropriate depreciation method, or in the asset's estimated useful life or residual value

Capital Expenditures during Useful Life
Ordinary repairs are costs to maintain an asset's operating efficiency and expected productive life. Such repairs are usually fairly small amounts that occur frequently and are debited to Repair (or Maintenance) Expense as they occur. They are called operating expenditures.

Additions and improvements are costs incurred to increase an asset's operating efficiency, productive capacity, or expected useful life. These costs are usually large and do not occur often. They increase the company's ability to produce and are capital expenditures. Capital expenditures are debited to the original asset account to which they relate (capitalized) and are depreciated over the remaining life of that asset.

Impairments
Fair value is normally not relevant since property, plant, and equipment are not purchased for resale, but rather for use in operations over the long term. Property, plant, and equipment are considered impaired if the asset's carrying amount exceeds its recoverable amount (the higher of the asset's fair value less costs to sell, or its value in use). If this is the case, an impairment loss must be recorded. An impairment loss is the amount by which the asset's carrying amount exceeds its recoverable amount.

Companies are required to review their assets regularly for possible impairment or do so whenever a change in circumstances affects an asset's recoverable amount. For example, if a machine has become obsolete, or if the market for a product made by a machine has dried up or has become very competitive, there is strong possibility that an impairment loss exists. Management is then required to estimate the machine's recoverable amount.

For example, on December 31, 2011, the Butler Company had on its books a computer that cost $30,000. The accumulated depreciation of the asset was $15,000. On that date, the computer's recoverable amount was $5,000. The entry to record the loss is as follows:

Dec. 31   Loss on Impairment   10,000
                Accumulated Depreciation—Equipment   10,000
          To record impairment loss on computer.

Note that the asset account is not used and the original cost of the asset is kept at its historical cost. The carrying amount will reflect the recoverable amount ($30,000 − $25,000), $5,000. The Accumulated Depreciation account can now include more than just the depreciation recorded on the asset to date. It will also include impairment losses, if there have been any. Future depreciation calculations will need to be revised because of the reduction in the asset's carrying amount.

Assuming that the asset will continue to be used in operations, the impairment loss is reported on the income statement as part of operating profit rather than as "other expense."

International Financial Reporting Standards allow the reversal of a previously recorded impairment loss. Traditionally, Canadian standards have not permitted companies to do this. Under IFRS, at each year end, the company must determine whether or not an impairment loss still exists by measuring the asset's recoverable amount. If this recoverable amount exceeds the current carrying amount, then a reversal is recorded. The reversal for an asset is limited to the amount required to increase the asset's carrying amount to what it would have been if the impairment loss had not been recorded. The reversal will result in additional revisions to depreciation calculations.

Cost Model versus Revaluation Model
Under IFRS, companies can choose to account for their property, plant, and equipment under either the cost model or the revaluation model. Only about 3% of companies reporting under IFRS use the revaluation model. The revaluation model is allowed under IFRS mainly because it is particularly useful in countries that experience high rates of inflation or for companies in certain industries, such as investment or real estate companies, where fair values are more relevant than cost.

Under the **revaluation model**, the carrying amount of property, plant, and equipment is its fair value less any subsequent accumulated depreciation less any subsequent impairment losses. This model can be applied only to assets whose fair value can be reliably measured, and revaluations must be carried out often enough that the carrying amount is not materially different from the asset's fair value at the balance sheet date. The accounting in the revaluation model is relatively complex, so few companies will use this model.

Changes in Depreciation Method, Estimated Useful Life, or Residual Value
The depreciation method used should be consistent with the pattern in which the asset's future economic benefits are expected to be consumed by the company. The appropriateness of the method should be reviewed at least annually in case there has been a change in the expected pattern. Management must also review its estimates of the useful life and residual value of the company's depreciable assets at least at each year end. If wear and tear or obsolescence indicates that the estimates are too low or too high, the estimates should be changed. If the depreciation method, the estimated useful life, or residual values are changed, this will cause a revision to the depreciation calculations.

Revised Depreciation Calculations
Revision of depreciation is a change in an estimate. The reason for this is that the original calculation of depreciation is based on the best information available at that time. The revision is based on new information; depreciation expense is revised for current and future years. There is no correction of previously recorded depreciation expense.

For example, the Forrester Company has an asset, bought on January 1, 2009, which cost $20,000. At the date the asset was purchased, it had an estimated residual value of $4,000, and a useful life of four years. On January 1, 2011, the asset's estimated useful life was reviewed and was increased by two years. There was no change in the estimated residual value. The asset had been depreciated using the straight-line method. The revised depreciation is calculated as follows:

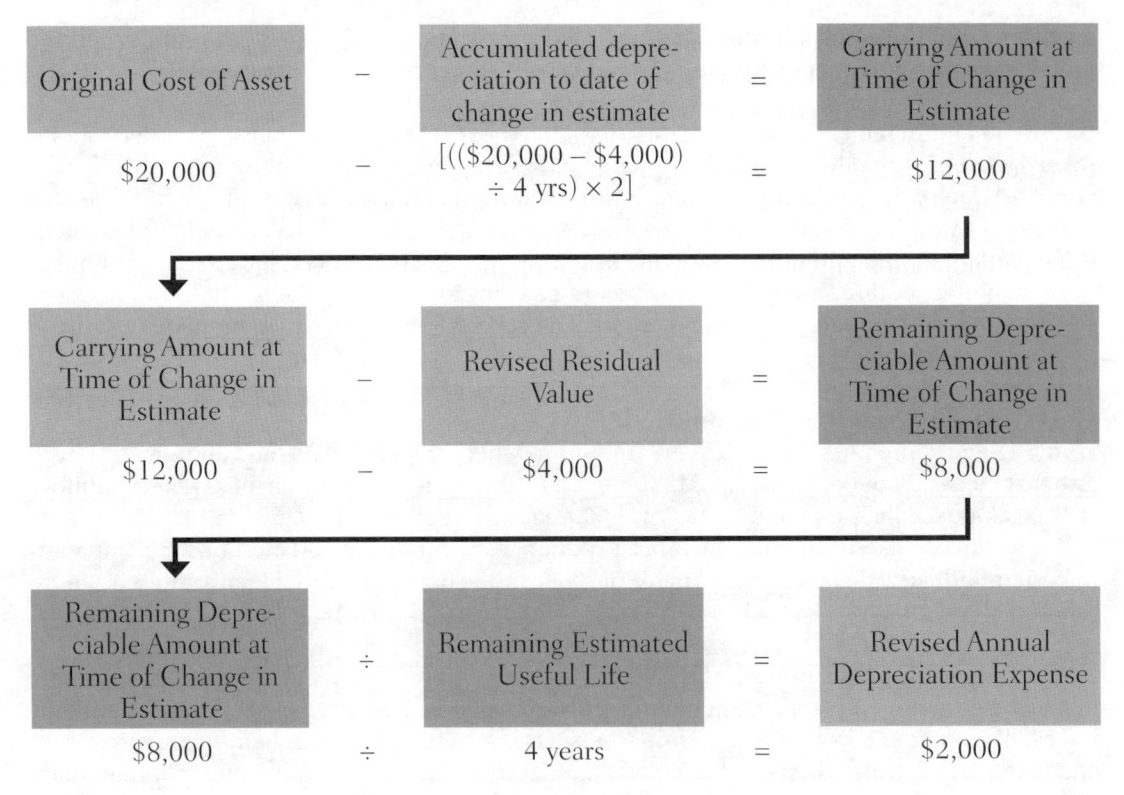

```
Original Cost of Asset  −  Accumulated depre-     =  Carrying Amount at
                           ciation to date of        Time of Change in
                           change in estimate        Estimate

      $20,000         −  [(($20,000 − $4,000)    =       $12,000
                           ÷ 4 yrs) × 2]
```

```
Carrying Amount at      Revised Residual          Remaining Depre-
Time of Change in   −   Value              =      ciable Amount at
Estimate                                          Time of Change in
                                                  Estimate

   $12,000          −       $4,000         =         $8,000
```

```
Remaining Depre-                                  Revised Annual
ciable Amount at    ÷   Remaining Estimated  =    Depreciation Expense
Time of Change in       Useful Life
Estimate

   $8,000           ÷       4 years        =         $2,000
```

Depreciation can be revised regardless of which method of depreciation is used. If the units-of-production method is used, the remaining estimate of useful life is expressed in units. If the diminishing-balance method is used, the revised rate would be applied to the carrying amount at the time of the change in estimate.

Disposals of Property, Plant, and Equipment

Study objective 4

Account for the disposal of property, plant, and equipment.

Property, plant, and equipment may be disposed of by retirement, sale, or exchange when an item is no longer useful to the company. Four steps are required to record the disposal of an asset.

Step 1: Update depreciation.
If the disposal occurs within the accounting period, depreciation must be updated for the fraction of the year since the last time adjusting entries were recorded up to the date of disposal.

Step 2: Calculate the carrying amount.
The carrying amount must be calculated after the accumulated depreciation is updated in Step 1.

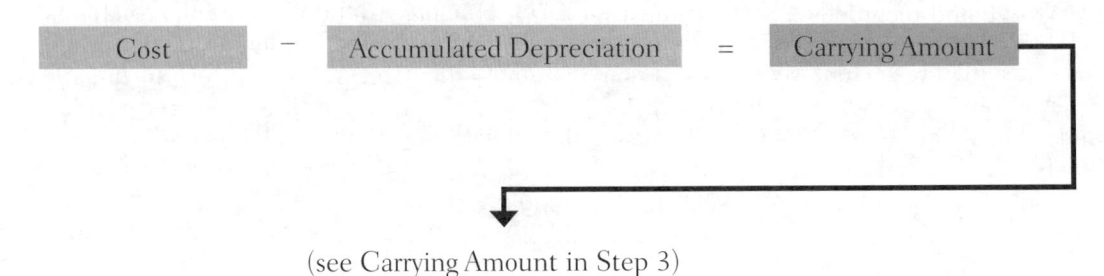

```
Cost    −    Accumulated Depreciation    =    Carrying Amount
```

(see Carrying Amount in Step 3)

Step 3: Calculate the gain or loss.
Determine the amount of the gain or loss on disposal, if any, by comparing the proceeds received from the disposal with the carrying amount at the date of disposal:

| Proceeds | − | Carrying Amount | = | Gain (Loss) |

If the proceeds of the sale are more than the carrying amount of the property, plant, or equipment, there is a gain on disposal. If the proceeds of the sale are less than the carrying amount of the asset sold, there is a loss on disposal.

Step 4: Record the disposal.
Recording the disposal of the asset means removing the asset from the accounts. The cost of the asset and the accumulated depreciation related to the asset are removed by crediting the asset account and debiting the accumulated depreciation account. The proceeds (if any) and the gain or loss (if any) are recorded. A gain on disposal is recorded as a credit; a loss on disposal is recorded as a debit.

> Dr. Cash (or other account)
> Dr. Accumulated Depreciation
> Dr. Loss on Disposal **OR** Cr. Gain on Disposal
>   Cr. Property, Plant, and Equipment

Gains and losses are reported in the operating section of a multiple-step income statement. Loss results when the annual depreciation expense has not been sufficient so that the carrying amount at the date of disposal is equal to the proceeds. Gains are caused because annual depreciation expense has been too high, so the carrying amount at the date of disposal is less than the proceeds. Thus gains and losses are basically just adjustments to depreciation expense and should be recorded in the same section of the income statement.

Retirement of Property, Plant, and Equipment
Disposal by retirement occurs when an asset is at the end of its useful life and the company no longer needs it. When an asset is retired, there are no proceeds on disposal. The Accumulated Depreciation account is decreased (debited) for the full amount of the depreciation taken over the life of the asset. The asset account is reduced (credited) for the asset's original cost.

For example, on November 30, the Perez Company retires a machine with a cost of $24,000 and accumulated depreciation of $22,000 to the date of disposal. The machine has no residual value and Perez Company does not receive any proceeds from the disposal of the asset. The entry to record the disposal is as follows:

Nov. 30	Accumulated Depreciation—Equipment	22,000	
	Loss on Disposal	2,000	
	Equipment		24,000
	To record retirement of machine at a loss.		

Even if the carrying amount equals zero, a journal entry is still required to remove the asset and its related depreciation account from the books.

Sale of Property, Plant, and Equipment

In a disposal by sale, the four steps listed earlier are followed. The asset's carrying amount is compared with the fair value (proceeds) received from the sale. If the sale proceeds exceed the carrying amount, a gain on disposal occurs. If the sale proceeds are less than the asset's carrying amount, a loss on disposal occurs.

Gain on Disposal. On September 30, Perez Company sells a machine with a cost of $24,000 and accumulated depreciation of $22,000 to the date of disposal, for $5,000 cash. The sale results in a $3,000 gain to Perez because the proceeds ($5,000) are greater than the carrying amount ($2,000) of the machine. The journal entry to record the sale is as follows:

Sept. 30	Cash	5,000	
	Accumulated Depreciation—Machine	22,000	
	Machine		24,000
	Gain on Disposal		3,000
	To record sale of machine at a gain.		

Loss on Disposal. Instead, on September 30, Perez Company sells the machine described above for $500 cash. The sale results in a $1,500 loss because the proceeds ($500) are $1,500 less than the carrying amount ($2,000) of the machine. The journal entry to record the sale is as follows:

Sept. 30	Cash	500	
	Accumulated Depreciation—Machine	22,000	
	Loss on Disposal	1,500	
	Machine		24,000
	To record sale of machine at a loss.		

Exchanges of Property, Plant, and Equipment

Sometimes an old asset may be exchanged for a new asset. An old asset may be traded in for a new one and a trade-in allowance may be granted toward the purchase price of the new asset. Cash may also be involved. The new asset is seen as being purchased for cash plus the value of the old asset. The trade-in allowance amount, however, is often affected by price concessions for the new asset and therefore rarely reflects the fair value of the asset that is given up. Consequently, as fair value is what matters, trade-in allowances are ignored for accounting purposes.

Instead of using the stated purchase price, the new asset is recorded at the fair value of the asset given up plus any cash paid (or less any cash received). Instead of using the trade-in allowance, the fair value of the asset given up is used to calculate the gain or loss on the asset being given up. A loss results if the carrying amount of the asset being given up is more than its fair value. A gain results if the carrying amount is less than its fair value.

The procedure to account for exchanges of assets is as follows:
Step 1: Update any unrecorded depreciation expense on the asset being given up to the date of the exchange.
Step 2: Calculate the carrying amount of the asset being given up (cost – accumulated depreciation).
Step 3: Calculate any gain or loss on disposal [fair value – carrying amount = gain (loss)].

Step 4: Record the exchange as follows:
- Remove the cost and the accumulated depreciation of the asset that is given up.
- Record any gain or loss on disposal.
- Record the new asset at the fair value of the old asset plus any cash paid (or less any cash received).
- Record the cash paid or received.

Natural Resources

Natural resources consist of standing timber and underground deposits of oil, gas, and minerals. These assets are frequently called **wasting assets** because they are physically extracted in mining, cutting, or pumping operations and can only be replaced by an act of nature.

> Study objective 5
> Calculate and record depreciation of natural resources.

Cost

The cost of acquiring a natural resource is determined the same way as the cost of property, plant, and equipment. It can also be increased by future removal and site restoration cleanup costs, which are large. These costs, known as retirement obligations, are usually required to return the resource as closely as possible to its natural state at the end of its useful life.

Depreciation

The units-of-production method is generally used to calculate the depreciation of wasting assets. Since natural resource depreciation is generally a function of the units extracted during a given period, the depreciable amount per unit of product is multiplied by the number of units extracted to calculate depreciation expense. The formula for calculating depreciation expense is the same as the units-of-production method illustrated earlier.

For example, assume that Nubal Mining Company invests $5.5 million in a mine that is estimated to have 10 million tonnes of uranium and a $200,000 residual value. In the first year, 800,000 tonnes of uranium are extracted. The following illustration shows the formulas and calculations.

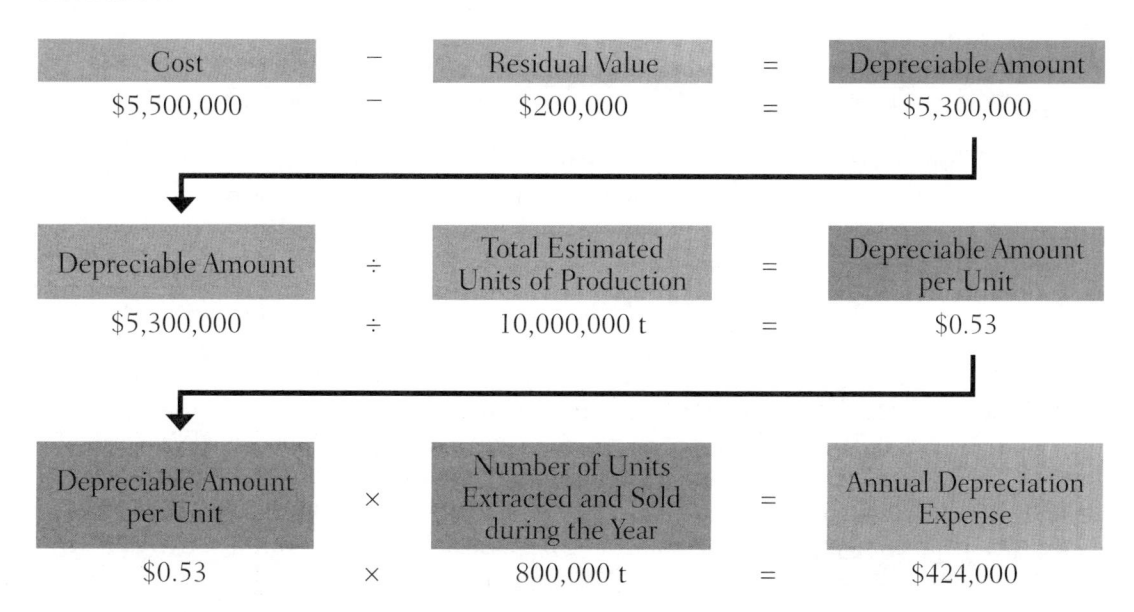

Cost	−	Residual Value	=	Depreciable Amount
$5,500,000	−	$200,000	=	$5,300,000

Depreciable Amount	÷	Total Estimated Units of Production	=	Depreciable Amount per Unit
$5,300,000	÷	10,000,000 t	=	$0.53

Depreciable Amount per Unit	×	Number of Units Extracted and Sold during the Year	=	Annual Depreciation Expense
$0.53	×	800,000 t	=	$424,000

However, the entry to record depreciation of the natural resource is different from the entry for the units-of-production method.

The entry to record the depreciation of Nubal for the period is as follows:

Dec. 31	Inventory	424,000	
	Accumulated Depreciation—Mines		424,000
	To record depreciation expense on mines.		

All costs of extracting the natural resource are recorded as inventory. When the resource extracted is sold, the inventory is reduced and the cost of goods sold is recorded and matched with the period's revenue.

The depreciable amount per unit of a natural resource may be revised if new information becomes available and the estimates need to be revised. Natural resources are also reviewed and tested for impairment whenever circumstances make this appropriate.

Disposal of Natural Resources

Before disposal of the natural resource, the depreciation must be recorded to the date of disposal. The proceeds are recorded, the cost and the accumulated depreciation of the natural resource are removed, and any gain or loss is recorded.

Intangible Assets

Study objective 6

Identify the basic accounting issues for intangible assets and goodwill.

Intangible assets provide future benefits through the special rights, privileges, and competitive advantage they convey. They have no physical characteristics and may arise from the following sources:
1. Government grants such as patents, copyrights, contracts, trademarks, and trade names
2. An acquisition of another business in which the purchase price includes a payment for goodwill
3. Private monopolistic arrangements arising from contractual agreements such as franchises and leases

An intangible asset must be identifiable, which means it must meet one of the two following criteria: (1) it can be separated from the company and sold whether or not the company intends to do so, or (2) it is based on contractual or legal rights, regardless of whether or not it can be separated from the company. Since goodwill cannot be separated from a company and sold, there are differences in the accounting for goodwill versus other intangible assets.

Accounting for Intangible Assets

Companies have a choice of following the cost model or the revaluation model when accounting for intangible assets subsequent to acquisition. Under the cost model, if an intangible asset has a finite (limited) life, its cost must be systematically allocated over its useful life. We called this "depreciation" when discussing tangible assets. With intangible assets, we use the term amortization.

Intangible assets are recorded at cost, which includes all costs of acquisition and other costs necessary to make the intangible ready for its intended use. Intangibles may have a limited useful life or an indefinite useful life. If an intangible asset has a limited useful life, its amortizable amount (cost minus residual value) is allocated over the shorter of its estimated useful life or its legal life. The useful life is usually shorter than the legal life, so useful life is most often used as the amortization period.

Companies must use the amortization method that best matches the pattern with which the asset's future economic benefits are expected to be consumed. If that pattern cannot be determined reliably, the straight-line method should be used.

If an intangible asset has an indefinite life, it is not amortized. However, the asset cost is reviewed and tested for impairment whenever circumstances make this appropriate. If the asset's recoverable amount permanently declines below its carrying value, impairment has occurred. An impairment loss should be recorded and the intangible asset written down to its recoverable amount. At disposal, the carrying value of the intangible asset is eliminated, and any gain or loss is recorded.

Intangible Assets with Finite Lives

Patents
A patent is an exclusive right issued by the Canadian Intellectual Property Office of Industry Canada that enables the recipient to manufacture, sell, or otherwise control an invention for a period of 20 years from the date of the application. The initial cost of a patent is the cash or cash equivalent price paid when the patent is acquired.

If there is an infringement of a patent, the legal costs incurred to successfully defend it are added to the Patent account and amortized over the patent's remaining useful life. The legal costs are considered necessary to prove the patent's validity.

The cost of the patent should be amortized over its legal life (20 years) or useful life, whichever is shorter.

Copyrights
Copyrights give the owner the exclusive right to reproduce and sell an artistic or published work. Copyrights in Canada extend for the life of the creator plus 50 years. The cost of a copyright includes the cost of acquiring and defending it and should be amortized over its legal life or its useful life, whichever is shorter. Generally its useful life is shorter than its legal life.

Research and Development Costs
Research and development (R&D) costs are not intangible assets in themselves, but R&D costs lead to patents and copyrights, new processes, and new products. Research and development costs present two accounting problems: (1) it is sometimes difficult to determine the costs related to specific projects; (2) it is also hard to know the extent and timing of future benefits.

Accounting distinguishes between research costs and development costs. Research is planned production to gain new knowledge and understanding. All research costs should be expensed when incurred. Development is the use of research findings and knowledge for a plan or design.

Development costs with reasonably certain future benefits should be capitalized. All of the following conditions must be met for development costs to be capitalized:
- Management must have the technical feasibility, intention, and ability to complete the intangible asset and use or sell it.
- A future market must be defined.
- Adequate resources must exist to complete the project.
- Management must be able to measure the costs related to the development of the intangible asset.

If any of these conditions are not met, the development costs must be expensed.

Intangible Assets with Indefinite Lives

An intangible asset is considered to have an indefinite life when there is no foreseeable limit to the length of time over which the asset is expected to generate cash. Trademarks and trade names, franchises and licences, and goodwill are intangible assets with indefinite lives. Sometimes they have finite lives and should be amortized over the shorter of their legal or useful lives.

Trademarks and Trade Names
A trademark or trade name is a word, phrase, jingle, or symbol that identifies a particular enterprise or product. Because they create immediate product identification, they help the sale of a product or service. In most cases, companies renew their trademarks or trade names every 15 years, so the trademark or trade name may have an indefinite useful life for as long as it remains marketable.

If the trademark or trade name is purchased, the cost is the purchase price. If the trademark or trade name is developed internally rather than purchased, it cannot be recognized as an intangible asset on the balance sheet.

Franchises and Licences
A franchise is a contractual arrangement between a franchisor and a franchisee. The franchisor gives the franchisee permission to sell certain products, offer specific services, or use certain trademarks or trade names.

Another type of franchise, granted by a government body, permits the enterprise to use public property in performing its services. These operating rights are called **licences**. An example is the use of airwaves for radio and TV broadcasting.

All costs that can be identified with the acquisition of the franchise or licence should be recognized. Accounting for these costs depends on the useful life of the franchise or licence. Annual payments made by franchisee to the franchisor in proportion to sales are called royalties.

Goodwill
Goodwill is the value of all favourable attributes that relate to a company. These include exceptional management, desirable location, good customer relations, skilled employees, high-quality products, fair pricing policies, and harmonious relations with labour unions.

Goodwill cannot be sold individually as it is part of the business as a whole. It is recorded only when there is a purchase of an entire business. It is recorded as the excess of cost (purchase price) over the fair value of the net assets (assets less liabilities) acquired. Goodwill has an indefinite life and is not amortized.

Both goodwill and indefinite-life intangible assets must be tested annually for impairment regardless of whether there is any indication of impairment. This is different than finite-life intangible assets, which are assessed for indications of impairment at the end of each year, and are tested only if the assessment shows that impairment may exist.

Impairment losses on goodwill are never reversed, even if the value of the company increases after the impairment loss has been recognized. But IFRS does allow for reversals of impairment losses on both finite-life and other indefinite-life intangible assets if their value increases in the future.

Statement Presentation and Analysis

Presentation

Property, plant, equipment, and natural resources are combined and reported on the balance sheet as "property, plant, and equipment" or "capital assets." Intangible assets are normally listed separately, following property, plant, and equipment. Goodwill must be disclosed separately.

> **Study objective 7**
> Illustrate the reporting and analysis of long-lived assets.

For assets that are depreciated or amortized, balances and the accumulated depreciation and/or amortization should be disclosed on the balance sheet or in the notes to the financial statements. The depreciation and amortization methods used should be described and the amount of depreciation and amortization expense for the period should also be disclosed. For assets that are not depreciated or amortized, the carrying amount of each major type of asset should be disclosed in the balance sheet or notes.

Impairment losses, if any, should be shown on a separate line on the income statement, with details disclosed in a note to the financial statement.

An example balance sheet follows:

SAMPLE COMPANY
Balance Sheet (partial)
December 31, 2011
(in thousands)

Assets

Rental equipment (note 3)	$ 88,641
Property, plant, and equipment (note 3)	70,130
Intangible assets	7,812
Goodwill	126,146

Sample Company would provide additional details on the long-lived assets in the notes to its financial statements. For example, note 3 would disclose the cost, accumulated depreciation, and carrying amount of Sample Company's property, plant, and equipment, which include land, buildings, equipment, assets under construction, assets held for sale, and its rental equipment.

Under IFRS, companies will also have to disclose if they are using the cost or the revaluation model for each class of assets, and include a reconciliation of the carrying amount at the beginning and end of the period for each class of long-lived assets in the notes to the financial statements. This means they must show all of the following for each class of long-lived assets: (1) additions, (2) disposals, (3) depreciation or amortization, (4) impairment losses, and (5) reversals of impairment losses. If a company uses the revaluation model, it must also disclose any increases or decreases from revaluations as well as other information about the revaluation.

Analysis

Two ratios to assess the profitability of total assets will be used: asset turnover and return on assets.

Asset Turnover
The asset turnover ratio indicates how efficiently a company uses its assets. It shows the dollars of sales produced for each dollar invested in assets. It is calculated as follows:

Net Sales	÷	Average Total Assets	=	Asset Turnover
$1,346,758	÷	($689,460 + $754,964) ÷ 2	=	1.86 times

The asset turnover ratio shows that each dollar invested in assets produced $1.86 in sales.

Return on Assets
The return on assets ratio measures overall profitability. It focuses on profit, showing the amount of profit generated by each dollar invested in assets. It is calculated as follows:

Profit	÷	Average Total Assets	=	Return on Assets
$29,325	÷	($689,460 + $754,964) ÷ 2	=	4.1%

As with other ratios, the return on assets should be compared with previous years, with other companies in the same industry, and with industry averages, to determine how well the company has performed.

Demonstration Problem (SO 1, 2, & 4)

On January 1, 2011, Hume Company purchases a machine that has a cash price of $7,000, freight charges of $250, insurance during transit of $50, assembly costs of $150, and a licence of $35 per year. Hume estimates that the machine will have a five-year useful life with an estimated residual value of $700.

Instructions
a. Prepare the entry for the purchase on January 1, 2011.
b. Prepare the entry to record depreciation to December 31, 2011, using the straight-line method.
c. Starting from January 1, 2011, and using the double diminishing-balance method, prepare a depreciation schedule using the information above.

d. Using the diminishing-balance schedule prepared in (c), record the sale of the asset on December 31, 2012, if the asset were sold for $5,000 cash.

Solution to Demonstration Problem

General Journal

	General Journal		J1
Date	Account Titles and Explanation	Debit	Credit
a.			
2011			
Jan. 1	Equipment	7,450	
	Licence Expense	35	
	Cash		7,485
	($7,000 + $250 + $50 + $150)		
b.			
Dec. 31	Depreciation Expense	1,350	
	Accumulated Depreciation—Equipment		1,350
	[($7,450 − $700) ÷ 5]		

Straight-line rate = 100% ÷ 5 = 20%

c. Calculation of double diminishing-balance rate:

Double diminishing-balance rate = 20% × 2 = 40%

Double Diminishing-Balance Depreciation Schedule

Year	Carrying Amount Beginning of the Year	Depreciation Rate	Depreciation Expense	End of Year Accumulated Depreciation	End of Year Carrying Amount
2011	$7,450	40%	$2,980	$2,980	$4,470
2012	4,470	40%	1,788	4,768	2,682
2013	2,682	40%	1,073	5,841	1,609
2014	1,609	40%	644	6,485	965
2015	965	40%	265*	6,750	700

*Depreciation expense for 2015 is $265 and not 40% of $965 because the asset cannot be depreciated below its residual value.

d.
2012
Dec. 31   Cash   5,000
        Accumulated Depreciation—Equipment   4,768
            Equipment   7,450
            Gain on Sale of Equipment   2,318
        To record sale of equipment.

Review Questions and Exercises

Multiple Choice

Circle the letter that best answers each of the following statements.

1. (SO 1 & 6) All of the following are descriptions of property, plant, and equipment except:

    a. long-lived assets.
    b. fixed assets.
    c. intangible assets.
    d. capital assets.

2. (SO 1) Property, plant, and equipment are often subdivided into four groups. Which of the following would not be classified as property, plant, and equipment?

    a. Land
    b. Land improvements
    c. Supplies
    d. Buildings

3. (SO 1) Plato Company acquired land with a purchase price of $150,000. Legal fees on acquisition were $6,000. Plato also incurred the following costs: demolition and removal of an old building, $4,000; grading and filling of land, $3,000; parking lot layout, $4,000. The land should be recorded at:

    a. $167,000.
    b. $150,000.
    c. $157,000.
    d. $163,000.

4. (SO 1) Land improvements include all of the following costs except:

    a. land survey.
    b. driveways.
    c. parking lots.
    d. fencing.

5. (SO 1) Mackenna Company purchased a delivery truck and incurred the following costs:

Cash price	$30,000
Painting of logo	600
Motor vehicle licence	75
Two-year accident insurance policy	700

    What amount should be recorded as the cost of the delivery truck?

    a. $30,000
    b. $30,600
    c. $30,675
    d. $31,300

6. (SO 1) Esmay Industries purchased real estate for $365,000. It paid $65,000 and took a mortgage in the amount of $300,000. Legal fees of $4,000 cash were also paid for the purchase. The real estate appraisal of the land was $375,000 and of the building was $200,000. The amount recorded in the Land account on recording the purchase is:

   a. $300,000.
   b. $365,000.
   c. $240,652.
   d. $375,000.

7. (SO 2) The factor that is not relevant in calculating depreciation is:

   a. replacement value.
   b. cost.
   c. residual value.
   d. useful life.

8. (SO 2) Using the straight-line method, depreciation expense is calculated as:

   a. (Cost ÷ Useful Life) − Residual Value.
   b. (Cost + Residual Value) ÷ Useful Life.
   c. (Cost − Residual Value) ÷ Useful Life.
   d. (Cost ÷ Useful Life) + Residual Value.

9. (SO 2) Bruno Company purchased equipment on January 1, 2011, at a total invoice cost of $280,000; additional costs of $5,000 for freight and $25,000 for installation were incurred. The equipment has an estimated residual value of $9,000 and an estimated useful life of five years. The amount of accumulated depreciation at December 31, 2012, if the straight-line method of depreciation is used, is:

   a. $98,000.
   b. $19,000.
   c. $120,400.
   d. $124,000.

10. (SO 2) Espinoza Enterprises purchased a truck for $27,000 on January 1, 2011. The truck will have an estimated residual value of $2,000 at the end of five years. Using the units-of-production method, the accumulated depreciation at December 31, 2012, can be calculated as:

    a. ($27,000 ÷ Total Estimated Production) × Units of Production for 2011.
    b. ($25,000 ÷ Total Estimated Production) × Units of Production for 2012.
    c. ($27,000 ÷ Total Estimated Production) × Units of Production for 2011 and 2012.
    d. ($25,000 ÷ Total Estimated Production) × Units of Production for 2011 and 2012.

11. (SO 2) The Newman Company purchased a machine on January 1, 2011, for $350,000. The machine has an estimated useful life of five years and a residual value of $50,000. The machine is being depreciated using the double diminishing-balance method. The carrying amount at December 31, 2012, is:

    a. $126,000.
    b. $158,000.
    c. $170,000.
    d. $224,000.

12. (SO 2) The depreciation method that normally charges the same amount to expense every year is:

    a. double diminishing-balance.
    b. capital cost allowance.
    c. straight-line.
    d. units-of-production.

13. (SO 2) The depreciable amount of an asset equals:

    a. recoverable value minus residual value.
    b. cost minus accumulated depreciation.
    c. cost minus residual value.
    d. cost minus depreciation expense.

14. (SO 2) Depreciation, for income tax purposes, is calculated using which of the following depreciation methods?

    a. Double diminishing-balance
    b. Single diminishing-balance
    c. Straight-line
    d. Units-of-production

15. (SO 2) The entry to record depreciation expense:

    a. decreases owner's equity and assets.
    b. decreases profit and increases liabilities.
    c. decreases assets and liabilities.
    d. decreases assets and increases liabilities.

16. (SO 3) Santana Company purchased a machine on January 1, 2011, for $8,000 with an estimated residual value of $2,000 and an estimated useful life of eight years. On January 1, 2013, Santana estimated that the machine will last 12 years from the date of purchase. The residual value is still estimated at $2,000. Using the straight-line method, the new annual depreciation will be:

    a. $450.
    b. $500.
    c. $600.
    d. $667.

17. (SO 3) Which of the following would be considered an ordinary repair?

    a. Constructing a new wing on a building
    b. Performing a major motor overhaul on a new truck
    c. Painting buildings
    d. Replacing a stairway with an escalator

18. (SO 3) Additions and improvements are:

    a. operating expenditures.
    b. debited to an appropriate asset account when they increase useful life.
    c. debited to accumulated depreciation when they do not increase useful life.
    d. debited to an appropriate asset account when they do not increase useful life.

19. (SO 3) Impairments occur when:

   a. an asset's recoverable value falls below its carrying value.
   b. the recoverable value falls but increases in future years.
   c. there is a permanent increase in the recoverable value of the asset.
   d. the asset loses value through obsolescence.

20. (SO 4) A long-lived asset may be disposed of by:

   a. retirement.
   b. sale.
   c. exchange.
   d. all of the above.

21. (SO 4) Equipment costing $27,000 was purchased on January 1, 2004. It was depreciated using the straight-line method based on a nine-year life with no residual value. On June 30, 2011, the equipment was discarded with no cash proceeds. What gain or loss should be recognized on the retirement?

   a. No gain or loss
   b. $6,000 loss
   c. $4,500 loss
   d. $3,000 gain

22. (SO 4) On January 1, Gardner Company sold a machine that had a carrying amount of $7,500 for $8,000 cash. The entry by Gardner Company on January 1 will include a:

   a. debit to Loss on Disposal.
   b. credit to Loss on Disposal.
   c. debit to Gain on Disposal.
   d. debit to Cash.

23. (SO 5) Natural resources include all of the following except:

   a. standing timber.
   b. land improvements.
   c. oil deposits.
   d. mineral deposits.

24. (SO 5) Abelard Company expects to extract 15 million tonnes of coal from a mine that cost $25 million. If no residual value is expected and 3 million tonnes are mined in the first year, the entry to record depreciation in the first year will include a:

   a. debit to Accumulated Depreciation of $3,000,000.
   b. credit to Depreciation Expense of $5,000,000.
   c. credit to Accumulated Depreciation of $5,000,000.
   d. debit to Depreciation Expense of $1,800,000.

25. (SO 6) All of the following are intangible assets except:

   a. franchises.
   b. copyrights.
   c. accounts receivable.
   d. goodwill.

26. (SO 6) A purchased patent has a remaining legal life of 15 years. It should:

   a. be expensed in the year of acquisition.
   b. be amortized over 15 years regardless of its useful life.
   c. be amortized over its useful life if less than 15 years.
   d. not be amortized.

27. (SO 6) Eloise Company incurred $350,000 in research costs in its laboratory to develop a patent granted on January 1, 2011. On July 31, 2011, Eloise paid $52,000 for legal fees to successfully defend the patent. The total amount debited to Patents through July 31, 2011, should be:

   a. $350,000.
   b. $52,000.
   c. $402,000.
   d. $298,000.

28. (SO 6) Goodwill from the acquisition of a business enterprise:

   a. should be expensed in the year of acquisition.
   b. is an asset that is subject to amortization.
   c. is an intangible asset.
   d. is granted by the federal government.

29. (SO 7) The balances of the major classes of property, plant, and equipment and accumulated depreciation should be disclosed:

   a. on bank loan applications.
   b. in the body of the balance sheet.
   c. in the notes to the financial statement.
   d. on the income tax return.

30. (SO 7) When calculating the asset turnover ratio, we divide net sales total by:

   a. total equity.
   b. average liabilities.
   c. total revenue.
   d. average total assets.

Matching

Match each term with its definition by writing the appropriate letter in the space provided.

Terms	Definitions
___ 1. Operating Expenditures	a. A depreciation method that applies a constant rate to the diminishing carrying amount of the asset over the useful life of the asset.
___ 2. Diminishing-balance method	b. Expenditures that are immediately charged against revenues as expenses.
___ 3. Natural resources	c. An exclusive right that enables the recipient to manufacture, sell, or otherwise control an invention for a period of 20 years from the date of application.

___ 4. Trade-in allowance

___ 5. Additions and improvements

___ 6. Ordinary repairs

___ 7. Units-of-production method

___ 8. Straight-line method

___ 9. Patent

___ 10. Intangible assets

___ 11. Copyright

___ 12. Depreciable amount

___ 13. Franchise

___ 14. Goodwill

___ 15. Trademark

d. A depreciation method in which the decline in service potential is attributable to production rather than time.

e. Is ignored for accounting purposes in exchanges of property, plant, and equipment.

f. Costs incurred to increase the operating efficiency, productive capacity, or expected productive life of property, plant, or equipment.

g. Expenditures to maintain the operating efficiency and productive life of the asset.

h. The amount paid for a business in excess of the net identifiable assets.

i. A depreciation method where the depreciation expense for the period is the same throughout the service life of the asset.

j. Rights, privileges, and competitive advantages that result from the ownership of long-lived assets that do not possess physical substance.

k. Expenditures that may lead to new products, processes, patents, and copyrights.

l. Long-lived assets that consist of standing timber and underground deposits of oil, gas, and minerals.

m. A word, phrase, or symbol that distinguishes or identifies a particular enterprise or product.

n. A right granted by the federal government giving the owner the exclusive right to reproduce and sell an artistic or published work.

o. A contractual agreement granting rights to sell certain products, render specific services, or use certain trademarks within a certain area.

___ 16. Research and development costs   p. The diminishing-balance method used to depreciate property, plant, and equipment as specified for income tax purposes.

___ 17. Capital cost allowance   q. The cost of a long-lived asset less its residual value.

Exercises

E9—1 (SO 1) During 2011, Bergson Company had the following property and equipment transactions:

Jan. 1 Purchased a bus for company tours. The bus had a purchase price of $123,000, plus costs of $500 for delivery charges, $500 for insurance during transit to the company, $4,000 for painting and lettering, $3,000 for a motor vehicle licence, and $6,000 for accident insurance for two years. Bergson Company paid $20,000 in cash and signed a Note Payable for the balance.

July 1 Purchased a factory machine and some office equipment for a total of $12,000 cash. The fair value of the factory machine was $9,000 and the fair value of the office equipment was $15,000.

Instructions
Journalize the transactions. Explanations are not necessary.

Date	General Journal		J1
	Account Titles	Debit	Credit
2011			

E9—2 (SO 1) On September 1, the Borzoa Company purchased real estate with a down payment of $69,000 cash and a mortgage of $300,000. The fair value of the land was $375,000 and the building was $200,000.

Instructions
a. Calculate the cost that should be allocated to each asset purchased.

b. Record the purchase of the real estate.

	General Journal		J1
Date	Account Titles and Explanation	Debit	Credit

E9—3 (SO 2) On January 1, 2011, Dewey Company purchased a delivery truck for $150,000. The delivery truck is estimated to have a $30,000 residual value after its four-year useful life. Total kilometres expected to be driven is 300,000. The truck was driven 95,000 kilometres in 2011, 100,000 kilometres in 2012, 105,000 kilometres in 2013.

Instructions
Fill in the appropriate amounts concerning the depreciation of the delivery truck under the depreciation methods identified below.

Straight-Line Method
   Calculation

Year	Carrying Amount Beginning of the Year	×	Depreciation Rate	=	Depreciation Expense	End of Year Accumulated Depreciation	End of Year Carrying Amount
2011	_____		_____		_____	_____	_____
2012	_____		_____		_____	_____	_____
2013	_____		_____		_____	_____	_____

Double Diminishing-Balance Method
   Calculation

Year	Carrying Amount Beginning of the Year	×	Depreciation Rate	=	Depreciation Expense	End of Year Accumulated Depreciation	End of Year Carrying Amount
2011	_____		_____		_____	_____	_____
2012	_____		_____		_____	_____	_____
2013	_____		_____		_____	_____	_____

Units-of-Production Method
   Calculation

Year	Kilometres Driven	×	Depreciable Amount / Unit	=	Depreciation Expense	End of Year Accumulated Depreciation	End of Year Carrying Amount
2011	_____		_____		_____	_____	_____
2012	_____		_____		_____	_____	_____
2013	_____		_____		_____	_____	_____

E9—4 (SO 4) During 2011, LeBarge Company had the following transactions related to its property, plant, and equipment. LeBarge Company normally records depreciation expense at the end of the annual fiscal year.

Jan. 1 A delivery truck costing $17,500, with accumulated depreciation of $6,500, is destroyed in an accident. The insurance company pays LeBarge $13,000.

July 1 Sold machinery costing $17,000 for $2,200 cash. The machinery had accumulated depreciation of $12,000 at December 31, 2010, based on annual depreciation of $2,000 per year.

Dec. 31 Retired a machine with a cost of $20,000 and accumulated depreciation of $18,000 to the end of 2010. The machine has been depreciated on the straight-line basis for nine years, with no estimated residual value. The machine has been used in the business throughout the entire year 2011 and is being retired at the end of the year.

Instructions
Journalize the transactions. Explanations are not necessary.

General Journal			J1
Date	**Account Titles**	**Debit**	**Credit**
2011			

E9—5 (SO 6) On December 31, 2010, the intangible asset section of Mill Company's balance sheet was:

Patents	$210,000	
Less: Accumulated amortization	13,000	$197,000
Franchise	120,000	
Less: Accumulated amortization	48,000	72,000
Copyrights	60,000	
Less: Accumulated amortization	48,000	12,000
Total intangibles		$281,000

Mill owns two patents: one purchased for $50,000 on January 1, 2010, with a total useful life of 10 years, and the other purchased for $160,000 on January 1, 2010, with a total useful life of 20 years. The franchise was obtained on January 1, 2005, for $120,000 and is being amortized over its contract life of 15 years. The copyrights were capitalized on January 1, 2007, at a cost of $60,000 and are being amortized over five years. During 2011, Mill purchased a patent on July 1 at a cost of $72,000. This patent has an estimated economic life of 12 years from July 1, 2011.

Instructions
Prepare the December 31, 2011, intangible assets section of Mill Company's balance sheet. Show all calculations for each intangible asset.

MILL COMPANY
Partial Balance Sheet
December 31, 2011

_____

_____

_____

_____

_____

_____

_____

_____

_____

E9—6 (SO 7) The Samora Company has given you the following information from its financial statements for the year ended December 31, 2011.

Total net sales	$1,220,567
Assets at beginning of year	$ 768,000
Assets at the end of year	$ 694,762
Profit for the year	$ 40,829

Calculate the following ratios:

a. The asset turnover for the year.

b. The return on assets for the year.

Solutions to Review Questions and Exercises

Multiple Choice

1. (c) Intangible assets are not included in property, plant, and equipment because they do not have physical substance. (a) Long-lived assets, (b) fixed assets, and (d) capital assets all refer to tangible assets.

2. (c) Property, plant, and equipment are subdivided into four classes: (1) Land, (2) Land improvements, (3) Buildings, and (4) Equipment. Supplies are classified as a current asset.

3. (d) The acquisition of land will consist of the purchase price ($150,000), lawyer's fee ($6,000), demolition and removal costs of an old building ($4,000), and grading and filling ($3,000), for a total of $163,000.

4. (a) Land survey costs are recorded in the Land account. Land improvements include driveways, parking lots, and fencing.

5. (b) The cost of a long-lived asset consists of all expenditures necessary to acquire the asset and make it ready for its intended use ($30,000 + $600 = $30,600). The payment for the licence is an annual recurring operating expenditure. The insurance premium is recorded as prepaid insurance and is expensed over its two-year life.

6. (c) The basket purchase of real estate was made at a total cost of $369,000. The total cost allocated to the Land account is calculated based on the appraisal of the land and the building. It is calculated as follows:

$$\frac{\$375,000}{\$575,000} \times \$369,000 = \$240,652$$

7. (a) Replacement value is not relevant in calculating depreciation.

8. (c) The formula for calculating depreciation expense under the straight-line method is (Cost − Residual Value) ÷ Useful Life.

9. (c) The cost of the equipment is $310,000 (the invoice cost of $280,000, freight costs of $5,000, and installation costs of $25,000). The annual depreciation is calculated as follows:

($310,000 − $9,000) ÷ 5 = $60,200 × 2 = $120,400

10. (d) The depreciable amount is $25,000 (cost of $27,000 minus residual value of $2,000). Accumulated depreciation must include the depreciation expense for both 2011 and 2012.

11. (a) Annual depreciation expense is calculated by multiplying the carrying amount at the beginning of the year by the diminishing-balance rate. Residual value is ignored until the end of the asset's useful life. The depreciation rate is double the straight-line rate of 20% or 20% × 2 = 40%.

Year	Carrying Amount Beginning of Year	Rate	Depreciation Expense	Carrying Amount End of Year
2011	$350,000	× 40% =	$140,000	$210,000
2012	$210,000	× 40% =	$ 84,000	$126,000

12. (c) The straight-line method of depreciation will normally result in the same amount of depreciation expense each year.

13. (c) The depreciable amount of an asset is equal to the cost of the asset less its residual value.

14. (b) Income tax regulations require the taxpayer to use the single diminishing-balance method. Depreciation is calculated on a class basis and is called capital cost allowance (CCA).

15. (a) The entry to record depreciation expense results in a debit to Depreciation Expense and a credit to Accumulated Depreciation. The debit to Depreciation Expense decreases profit and thus owner's equity. The credit to Accumulated Depreciation increases the contra asset account, which decreases the carrying amount of the asset to which it relates.

16. (a) To determine the new annual depreciation expense, the depreciable amount is divided by the revised remaining useful life as follows:

    Depreciation expense for 2011: ($8,000 − $2,000) ÷ 8 = $750
    Carrying amount at end of 2012: $8,000 − (2 × $750) = $6,500
    Remaining useful life: (12 − 2) = 10 years
    Revised annual depreciation for remaining 10 years: ($6,500 − $2,000) ÷ 10 = $450

17. (c) Ordinary repairs include motor tune-ups done on delivery trucks, replacing worn out tires, and painting buildings. Choices (a), (b), and (d) are additions and improvements to assets that increase the life of the asset and are considered capital expenditures.

18. (b) Additions and improvements are capital expenditures. When the expenditure increases useful life, it should be debited to an appropriate asset account.

19. (c) Property, plant, and equipment are considered impaired if the asset's carrying amount exceeds its recoverable amount.

20. (d) Property, plant, and equipment may be disposed of by retirement, sale, or exchange.

21. (c) On June 30, 2011, the asset would have a carrying amount of $4,500, as calculated below:

Cost	$27,000
Depreciation, 2004–2010 (7 × $3,000)	(21,000)
Depreciation, Jan. 1–June 30, 2011	(1,500)
(6/12 × $3,000)	
Carrying amount, June 30, 2011	$4,500

Since the asset was discarded with no cash proceeds, a loss of $4,500 should be recognized.

22. (d) The $8,000 cash is recorded with a debit to Cash, and since the amount of cash received is more than the asset's carrying amount, a gain would be recorded with a credit to Gain on Disposal.

23. (b) Natural resources consist of standing timber and underground deposits of oil, gas, and minerals. Land improvements are reported as tangible property, plant, and equipment.

24. (c) The calculation for depreciation using the units-of-production method is:

$$\frac{\$25,000,000}{15,000,000} = \$1.67 \text{ and } \$1.67 \times 3,000,000 = \$5,000 \text{ (rounded)}$$

The entry is as follows:

Inventory	5,000,000	
Accumulated Depreciation—Coal Mine		5,000,000

25. (c) Intangible assets are rights, privileges, and competitive advantages that result from the ownership of long-lived assets that do not possess physical substance. They include patents, copyrights, trademarks, trade names, franchises, licences, and goodwill. Accounts receivable is a current asset.

26. (c) The cost of a patent should be amortized over its legal life or useful life, whichever is shorter.

27. (b) The research costs of $350,000 should be expensed when incurred. The legal fees ($52,000) in successfully defending the patent are debited to the Patent account.

28. (c) Goodwill is an intangible asset that is recognized when the purchase price to acquire an entire business exceeds the recoverable value of the net assets acquired. Since goodwill does not have a legal life or an identifiable useful life, it is not subject to amortization.

29. (c) For assets that are depreciated, the balances and accumulated depreciation should be disclosed in notes to the financial statement.

30. (d) Asset turnover = Net sales total ÷ Average total assets.

Matching

1. b
2. a
3. l
4. e
5. f
6. g
7. d
8. i
9. c
10. j
11. n
12. q
13. o
14. h
15. m
16. k
17. p

Exercises

E9—1

General Journal			J1
Date	Account Titles	Debit	Credit
2011			
Jan. 1	Bus	128,000	
	Licence Expense	3,000	
	Prepaid Insurance	6,000	
	Cash		20,000
	Notes Payable		117,000
July 1	Factory Machinery	4,500	
	Office Equipment	7,500	
	Cash		12,000

E9—2

1. Total cost of real estate $369,000

    Value of real estate

    Land   375,000

    Building   200,000

    Total $575,000

    Land cost $\frac{375}{575} \times 369{,}000 = \$240{,}652$

    Building cost $\frac{200}{575} \times 369{,}000 = \$128{,}348$

2.

General Journal			J1
Date	Account Titles	Debit	Credit
Sept 1	Land	240,652	
	Building	128,348	
	Mortgage Payable		300,000
	Cash		69,000
	To record purchase of real estate.		

E9—3
Straight-Line Method

Year	Depreciable Amount		Depreciation Rate		Depreciation Expense	End of Year Accumulated Depreciation	End of Year Carrying Amount
2011	$120,000	×	25%	=	$30,000	$30,000	$90,000
2012	120,000	×	25%	=	30,000	60,000	60,000
2013	120,000	×	25%	=	30,000	90,000	30,000

Double Diminishing-Balance Method

Year	Depreciable Amount		Depreciation Rate		Depreciation Expense	End of Year Accumulated Depreciation	End of Year Carrying Amount
2011	$150,000	×	50%	=	$75,000	$75,000	$75,000
2012	75,000	×	50%	=	37,500	112,500	37,500
2013	37,000	×	50%	=	7,500*	120,000	30,000*

*Depreciation stops when the asset's carrying amount equals its residual value.

Units-of-Production Method

Year	Kilometres Driven		Depreciable Amount/Unit		Depreciation Expense	End of Year Accumulated Depreciation	End of Year Carrying Amount
2011	95,000	×	$0.40*	=	$38,000	$38,000	$112,000
2012	100,000	×	0.40	=	40,000	78,000	72,000
2013	105,000	×	0.40	=	42,000	120,000	30,000

*$150,000 − $30,000 = $120,000 ÷ 300,000 = $0.40 per unit

E9—4

General Journal			J1
Date	Account Titles	Debit	Credit
2011			
Jan. 1	Cash	13,000	
	Accumulated Depreciation—Truck	6,500	
	Truck		17,500
	Gain on Disposal		2,000
July 1	Depreciation Expense	1,000	

		Accumulated Depreciation—Machinery		1,000
		Cash	2,200	
		Accumulated Depreciation—Machinery	13,000	
		Loss on Disposal	1,800	
		Machinery		17,000
	Dec. 31	Depreciation Expense	2,000	
		Accumulated Depreciation—Machine		2,000
	Dec. 31	Accumulated Depreciation—Machine	20,000	
		Machine		20,000

E9—5

MILL COMPANY
Partial Balance Sheet
December 31, 2011

Intangible assets:		
Patents	$282,000	
Less: Accumulated amortization	29,000	$253,000*
Franchise	120,000	
Less: Accumulated amortization	56,000	64,000**
Copyrights	60,000	
Less: Accumulated amortization	60,000	0
Total intangibles		$ 317,000

Calculations:

*Patents:

$50,000	Jan. 1, 2010, 10 yrs, amortization to date = (Accumulated amortization: $5,000 × 2 years)	$10,000
+ 160,000	Jan. 1, 2010, 20 yrs, amortization to date = (Accumulated amortization: $8,000 × 2 years)	16,000
+ 72,000	July 1, 2006, 12 yrs, amortization to date = (Accumulated amortization: $6,000 × .5 years)	3,000
$ 282,000	Total amortization to date	$29,000

**Franchise:

$120,000, Jan. 1, 2005, 15 yrs, amortization to date = (Accumulated amortization: $8,000 × 7 years)	$56,000

Copyrights:

$60,000, Jan. 1, 2007, 5 yrs, amortization to date = (Accumulated amortization: $12,000 × 5 years)	$60,000

E9—6

Total net sales	$1,220,567
Assets at beginning of year	$ 768,000
Assets at the end of year	$ 694,762
Profit for the year	$ 40,829

1. The asset turnover for the year
   Net Sales ÷ Average Total Assets = Asset Turnover

   $1,220,567 ÷ [($768,000 + $694,762) ÷2] = 1.67

2. The return on assets for the year
   Profit ÷Average Total Assets = Return on Assets

   $40,829 ÷ [($768,000 + $694,762) ÷2] = 5.58%

chapter 10

Current Liabilities and Payroll

Study objectives >>

After studying this chapter, you should be able to:
1. Account for determinable or certain current liabilities.
2. Account for estimated liabilities.
3. Account for contingencies.
4. Determine payroll costs and record payroll transactions.
5. Prepare the current liabilities section of the balance sheet.
6. Calculate mandatory payroll deductions (Appendix 10A).

Preview of Chapter 10

Every company has current liabilities. A current liability is a debt that is expected to be settled within one year from the balance sheet date or in the company's normal operating cycle. We will explain current liabilities in this chapter. Payroll results in current liabilities and is also explained in this chapter. This chapter is organized as follows:

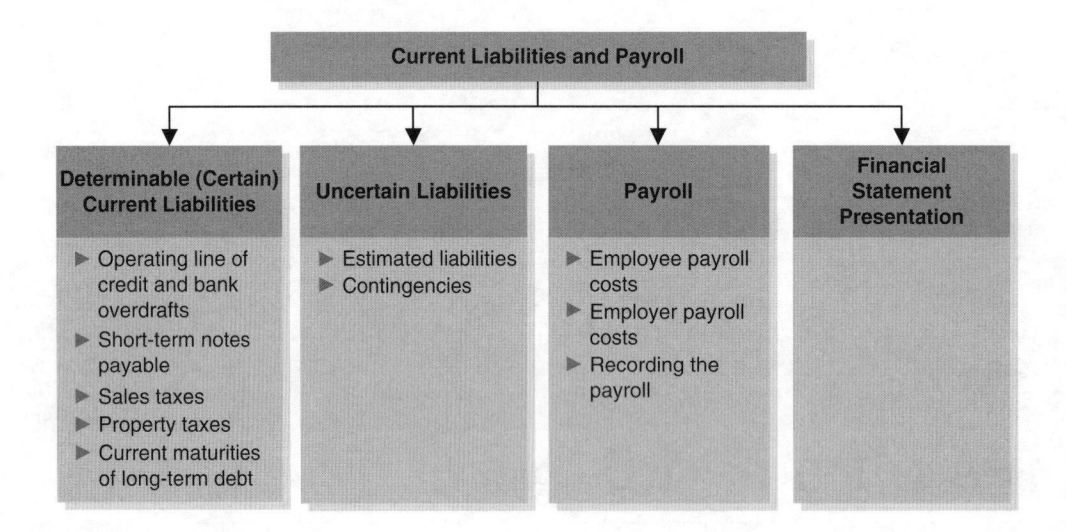

Current Liabilities and Payroll

- **Determinable (Certain) Current Liabilities**
  - Operating line of credit and bank overdrafts
  - Short-term notes payable
  - Sales taxes
  - Property taxes
  - Current maturities of long-term debt
- **Uncertain Liabilities**
  - Estimated liabilities
  - Contingencies
- **Payroll**
  - Employee payroll costs
  - Employer payroll costs
  - Recording the payroll
- **Financial Statement Presentation**

Determinable (Certain) Current Liabilities

Study objective 1

Account for determinable or certain current liabilities.

Liabilities are present obligations, arising from past events, to make future payments of assets or services. An essential characteristic of a liability is the existence of a present obligation. Sometimes there is a great deal of uncertainty regarding whether or not a liability exists. Even if it is certain that the liability exists, sometimes we are not certain whom we owe, how much we owe, or when the liability is due.

A determinable liability is one with a known amount, payee, and due date. Examples of determinable current liabilities include bank indebtedness from operating lines of credit, notes payable, accounts payable, sales taxes payable, unearned revenue, and current maturities of long-term debt. Also included in this category are accrued liabilities such as property taxes, payroll, and interest.

Operating Line of Credit and Bank Overdrafts

Operating Line of Credit
An operating line of credit is a pre-authorization from the bank to borrow money, up to a pre-set limit, when it is needed. A line of credit makes it very easy for a company to borrow money. The bank covers all cheques written by the company in excess of the company's bank account balance, up to the approved credit limit.

The line of credit is repayable upon request by the bank. Most companies borrow money, as needed, from the bank to meet short-term cash shortfalls. Security, called **collateral**, is usually required by the bank as protection in case the company is unable to repay the loan. Collateral normally includes some, or all, of the company's current assets (e.g., accounts receivable or inventories); investments; or property, plant, and equipment.

Bank Overdraft

Some companies have a negative, or overdrawn, cash balance at year end as a result of using their line of credit. This amount is usually called bank indebtedness, bank overdraft, or bank advances. The amount represents a liability of the company. Interest is charged on the overdrawn amount at a floating rate such as prime plus a specified percentage. The prime rate is the interest rate that banks charge their best customers. The overdraft is reported as a current liability, normally called bank indebtedness, with disclosure in the notes to the financial statements.

Short-term Notes Payable

Notes payable are obligations in the form of written promissory notes that usually require the borrower to pay interest monthly or at maturity. Notes payable may be used instead of accounts payable. This gives the lender proof of the obligation in case legal action is needed to collect the debt. Accounts and notes payable that result from purchase transactions (i.e., amounts owed to suppliers) are often called trade payables. Notes payable are also frequently issued to meet short-term financing needs.

Notes due for payment within one year of the balance sheet date are usually classified as current liabilities.

For example, Erhardt Company borrows $50,000 cash from Brentwood Bank on January 1, 2011, and signs a seven-month, 6% note payable. The entry to record this is as follows:

Jan. 1	Cash	50,000	
	Note Payable		50,000
	To record issue of seven-month, 6% note to Brentwood Bank.		

During the life of the note, interest payable must be accrued as an expense and be recorded in the period when the borrowed money is used. At the end of each month Erhardt Company will record the following:

Jan. 31	Interest Expense	250	
	Interest Payable		250
	To accrue interest for January. ($50,000 × 6% × 1/12)		

If Erhardt Company has a January 31 year end, the year-end financial statements will show notes payable of $50,000 and interest payable of $250 in the current liabilities section of the balance sheet. In addition, interest expense of $250 will be reported as other expenses in the income statement. Interest payable is shown separately from the note payable.

At maturity, Notes Payable is debited for the face value of the note, and Interest Payable is debited for accrued interest after interest is brought up to date. At the end of seven months Erhardt will record the following:

Aug. 1	Interest Expense	1,500	
	Interest Payable (6 × $250)		1,500
	To accrue interest from February to August.		

Aug. 1	Notes Payable	50,000	
	Interest Payable (7 × $250)	1,750	
	Cash		51,750
	To record payment of note and accrued interest.		

Sales Taxes

Sales taxes are expressed as a stated percentage of the sales price on goods sold to customers by a retailer. Sales taxes may take the form of Goods and Services Tax (GST), Provincial Sales Tax (PST), or Harmonized Sales Tax (HST). The entry by the retailer to record sales taxes is as follows:

Cash	XXXX	
Sales		XXXX
PST Payable		XXXX*
GST Payable		XXXX

GST is a federal tax assessed at 5% across Canada. HST is a combination of GST and PST, assessed at 13%, that is used in British Columbia, Ontario, Newfoundland and Labrador, Nova Scotia, and New Brunswick. Saskatchewan and Manitoba are also expected to harmonize their sales taxes in the near future.

*PST is a provincial tax with rates that vary from 0% to 10% among provinces across Canada. Alberta, Yukon, Northwest Territories, and Nunavut do not have PST. Quebec and Prince Edward Island are the only two provinces, with a separate provincial sales tax system, where there are currently no thoughts of harmonizing with the federal sales tax. Quebec sales tax is called the QST.

The amount of the sale and the amount of the sales tax collected are usually rung up separately on the cash register. The cash register readings are then used to credit sales or services and update the correct sales taxes payable accounts. If sales taxes are not rung up separately on the cash register, total receipts are divided by 100% plus the sales tax percentage to determine the sales at retail.

Sales taxes are not an expense (or revenue) of the retailer, but must be collected and forwarded to the appropriate government. The difference between the amount rung up and the sales at retail is the sales tax amount that is sent to the provincial or federal government annually, quarterly, or monthly.

Property Taxes

Property taxes, charged by municipal and provincial governments annually, are paid by businesses that own property. Tax bills received in March are usually payable by May or later in the year. The tax generally covers a calendar year.

Once the property tax bill has been received, the liability is recorded with the current and past month(s) expenses. For example, Maximus Company received its 2011 property tax bill in the amount of $3,600 on February 28, 2011. The entry on February 28, 2011, is as follows:

Feb. 28	Property Tax Expense	600	
	Property Tax Payable		600
	To record property tax expense for January and February 2011.		

When the business pays the annual property tax bill on April 30, 2011, the entry to record payment is as follows:

Apr. 30	Property Tax Payable	600	
	Property Tax Expense ($3,600 × 2/12)	600	
	Prepaid Property Tax ($3,600 × 8/12)	2,400	
	Cash		3,600
	To record property tax payment for 2011.		

After the payment, Maximus has a zero balance in its liability account but still has a prepayment. Since Maximus only makes adjusting entries annually, it would not adjust the prepaid property tax account until its year end, December 31. The entry to adjust the account on December 31 will be as follows:

Dec. 31	Property Tax Expense	2,400	
	Prepaid Property Tax		2,400
	To adjust property tax account to December 31, 2011.		

There are other acceptable ways to record and adjust property taxes. Some companies debit Property Tax Expense when the bill is recorded on March 1 and avoid a later adjusting entry. In addition, companies may prepare monthly or quarterly adjusting entries.

Current Maturities of Long-Term Debt

Current maturities of long-term debt occur when a company with long-term debt has a portion of that debt due in the current year. It is not necessary to prepare an adjusting journal entry to recognize the current debt. The current portion of the long-term debt is usually reclassified as a current liability when the balance sheet is prepared.

Uncertain Liabilities

In the previous section, we discussed current liabilities where there was a high degree of certainty regarding whom is owed, how much is owed, and when it is due. There was no uncertainty about the liability's existence, amount, or timing. In this section, we will discuss liabilities that have a lower degree of certainty but are still likely to occur. We will then discuss situations where it is unlikely that an obligation exists, or where the existence of a liability depends on the outcome of a future event.

Study objective 2: Account for estimated liabilities.

Estimated Liabilities

Estimated liabilities are liabilities that are known to exist but whose amount and timing are uncertain. The company knows it will owe someone but is not sure about how much and when the liability is due. There is a lower degree of certainty than in determinable liabilities, but as long as it is likely the company will have to settle the obligation, and the company can reasonably estimate the amount, it recognizes the liability. Common estimated liabilities include product warranties, customer loyalty programs, and gift cards.

Product Warranties

Product warranties (also known as guarantees) are promises made by sellers to buyers to replace or repair defective products within a specified time period following the date of the sale of the item. Warranties will lead to future costs for the manufacturer to repair or replace defective units.

Recording the estimated cost of product warranties as an expense and a liability in the period when the sale occurs also ensures companies have recognized the full cost of the sale in the period when the sale occurs. This is commonly known as matching expenses with revenues.

A warranty liability is an estimate of the possible number of warranty claims that will be made by customers, the expected cost to repair or replace the units, and the time in which the claims will be made. These estimates are based on a company's past experience.

For example, The Lee Company sells 50,000 freezers and estimates that 1% will be defective and the repair cost for each defective unit would average $50. On December 31, 2011, at the year end, the company will make the following journal entries related to the warranty liability:

Dec. 31	Warranty Expense	25,000	
	Warranty Liability		25,000
	To accrue estimated warranty costs.		
	(50,000 units × 1% × $50)		

Claims may be made by customers any time within the warranty period. If at the end of December 31, 2012, warranty claims totalled $15,000, the journal entry to record customer claims honoured is as follows:

Dec. 31	Warranty Liability	15,000	
	Repair Parts Inventory and/or Wages Payable		15,000
	To record honouring of warranty contracts on 2011 sales.		

The credit to Repair Parts Inventory is a reduction of the asset account, Inventory. The credit to Wages Payable will eventually reduce the Wages Expense. The accounts may be credited separately. If, after the specified time of the warranty, the actual warranty expense is not equal to the estimated liability amount, the warranty liability should be reviewed and adjusted as required.

Customer Loyalty Programs

Customer Loyalty Programs (also called promotions or incentive programs) take various forms and are offered by companies to attract or keep customers. They are designed to increase sales. When customer loyalty programs result in a reduction in the selling price of an item, it should be accounted for as a decrease in revenue and not as an expense.

Similar to product warranties, customer loyalty programs result in an estimated liability because companies do not know how many customers will redeem loyalty program offers and when the customer will do this. Therefore, customer loyalty program redemptions must be estimated in the same period that the sale is recorded. This estimate is recorded as a reduction to revenue and as a current liability.

For example, Rodger's Shop Rite has a rewards program where Rodger's Shop Rite customers get a redemption reward of five cents per litre of gasoline that can be used in Rodger's Shop Rite on the purchase of groceries. On July 31, the gas bar sells 12,500 litres of gasoline. Rodger's Shop Rite will record the following for the redemption rewards issued:

Jul. 1	Sales Discount for Redemption Rewards Issued	625	
	Redemption Rewards Liability		625
	To record redemption rewards issued on gasoline sales.		
	(12,500 × $0.05)		

Assume that on August 31, customers redeem $200 of the rewards in Rodger's Shop Rite when purchasing $8,500 of groceries. Rodger's Shop Rite makes the following entry that day (ignoring the cost of sales):

Aug. 31	Reward Redemptions Liability	200	
	Cash ($8,500 − $200)	8,300	
	Grocery Sales Revenue		8,500
	To record grocery sales and the redemption of rewards.		

Sales Discount for Redemption Rewards Issued is a contra sales account. Redemptions Rewards Liability is a current liability on the balance sheet.

Gift Cards

Gift cards or gift certificates are similar to unearned revenues in that the company receives cash in advance of providing the goods or the services. When gift cards are issued, an unearned revenue account (liability) is recorded. When the gift card is redeemed (used), the company will then record the sales or service revenue and reduce or debit the Unearned Revenue account.

The difficulty with gift cards is that it is unknown when and even if the card will be redeemed. The main accounting problem is: At what point should a company write off the gift card liability if it expects the gift card will never be redeemed? Recent changes to Canadian laws have prohibited expiry dates on gift cards. Theoretically, if the gift card has no expiration date, the company should indefinitely report the unused portion on the balance sheet as a liability.

If it is unlikely that the company will have to settle a portion of the liability, then an obligation no longer exists. As with warranties and customer loyalty programs, a company with a gift card program will need to estimate the appropriate balance for the liability. Currently, accounting standards do not give clear guidance on this issue.

Lawsuits

In some circumstances, lawsuits result in an estimated liability. If it is likely that the company will lose the lawsuit and if the amount can be reliably estimated, then the company must record a liability for the same reasons warranty liabilities are recorded. But lawsuits can involve a much higher degree of uncertainty than warranties. In that case, the accounting for a lawsuit is different than accounting for an estimated liability.

Contingencies

A contingency is an event with uncertain outcomes. It is not known whether the result from the situation would be a gain (and a related asset) or loss (and a related liability) until one or more events happen or do not happen. A gain will result in a related contingent asset and a loss in a related contingent liability. Both contingent assets and contingent liabilities, as well as required accounting and disclosure requirements, will be discussed in this section.

Study objective 3
Account for contingencies.

Contingent Liabilities

In the previous section we saw that liabilities are recorded even when estimations of the amount, timing, or the payee are required. As long as it is considered likely that a liability exists, and the amount can be reliably estimated, then it must be recorded.

In other circumstances, there is a higher degree of uncertainty as one or more of the criteria for recognizing liabilities are not met. These circumstances include the following:
- a *possible* (but not likely) obligation exists but will be confirmed only by the occurrence or non-occurrence of an uncertain future event,
- a present obligation exists but it is not probable that the company will have to settle it, and
- a present obligation exists but the amount cannot be reliably measured.

Under International Financial Reporting Standards (IFRS), if any one of these circumstances exists then it is called a **contingent liability**. Under IFRS, a company should not recognize a contingent liability in its balance sheet because it doesn't meet the definition of a liability. Contingent liabilities are disclosed only in the notes to the financial statements, unless the probability of occurrence is remote.

Under Canadian GAAP for Private Enterprises, contingent liabilities are viewed somewhat differently than under IFRS. Under Canadian GAAP for Private Enterprises, a contingent liability is defined as a liability that is contingent on the occurrence or non-occurrence of some future event. The contingent liability would be recorded if **both** of the following conditions are met:
1. The contingency is likely (the chance of occurrence is high).
2. The amount of the contingency can be reasonably estimated.

Under IFRS, a liability would also be recorded if both those conditions existed, but such a liability would be considered an estimated liability, not a contingent liability. For example, in the previous section we discussed how a lawsuit can be considered an estimated liability. Even though the existence of a liability is contingent on the outcome of the lawsuit, if it is likely the lawsuit will be lost, and the amount can be reliably estimated, it is considered an estimated liability.

Under IFRS, contingent liabilities are liabilities where there is too high of a degree of uncertainty to record the liability. Canadian GAAP for Private Enterprises considers a liability to be a contingent liability as long as its ultimate existence depends on the outcome of a future event, even if the event is likely to occur. Thus a lawsuit would be considered a contingent liability under Canadian GAAP for Private Enterprises.

The differences between IFRS and Canadian GAAP for Private Enterprises are to a certain extent based on semantics because of the different definitions of contingent liabilities. But it is still important to understand the distinction as private companies will have the choice to follow Canadian GAAP for Private Enterprises or IFRS, while public companies must follow IFRS.

The IFRS rule of never recording contingent liabilities may sound less strict than Canadian GAAP for Private Enterprises, where sometimes contingent liabilities are recorded. But in fact, IFRS is generally regarded as having a lower threshold for recognizing liabilities. Under IFRS, estimated liabilities are recognized for probable events, defined as being more likely than not. Under Canadian GAAP for Private Enterprises, only highly likely contingent liabilities are recognized.

For example, if a company is sued by a customer for $500,000, the amount the company will have to pay depends on a court decision that would only be known if and when a judge decides that the company owes the customer and how much it owes. If the judge decides in the company's favour, the company would owe the customer nothing. The company's liability is contingent on the judge's decision—a future event.

Contingent Assets

Contingent assets arise from past events where the asset's existence will be recognized only when a future event occurs or does not occur. This event will confirm the existence of a future cash inflow or other economic benefits that will result in an asset. Contingent assets are never recorded or accrued in the financial statements. They are disclosed in the notes to the financial statements only if it is likely that a gain will be realized.

Under IFRS, if it is virtually certain that a gain will occur, the related asset is not considered a contingent asset. It is simply considered to be an asset and is recognized in the financial statements as appropriate. Under Canadian GAAP for Private Enterprises, a contingent asset can be recognized only when the contingency is resolved and the asset is realized. Under both standards, it is not considered appropriate to disclose the existence of a contingent asset that, in management's opinion, is unlikely to occur.

Payroll

There are two types of payroll costs to a company: employee costs and employer costs. The first type, employee costs, involves the gross amount earned by employees. The second type, employer costs, involves amounts paid by the employer on behalf of the employee (employee benefits). Every employer has three types of payroll liabilities related to employees' salaries or wages: (1) the net pay owed to employees, (2) employees' payroll deductions, and (3) employer payroll deductions.

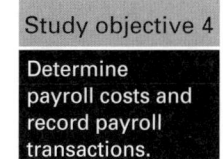

> **Study objective 4**
> Determine payroll costs and record payroll transactions.

Employee Payroll Costs

Determining payroll costs for employees involves calculating (1) gross pay, (2) payroll deductions, and (3) net pay.

Gross Pay

Gross earnings is the total compensation earned by an employee. It consists of wages or salaries, plus any bonuses and commissions.

Total wages are determined by multiplying the hours worked by the hourly rate of pay. Most companies are required to pay a minimum of one and one-half times the regular hourly rate for overtime hours worked. The number of hours worked before overtime is payable varies by industry and occupation.

Salary is based on a weekly, biweekly, monthly, or yearly rate. Most executive and administrative positions are salaried and do not earn overtime pay.

Payroll Deductions

Total payroll deductions (sometimes called withholdings) is the difference between gross pay and amount the employee actually receives. It is not an expense to the employer. The employer withholds the deduction and later pays it to the government and other agencies. Deductions may be mandatory (required by law) or voluntary (requested by the employee).

Mandatory Payroll Deductions. These deductions are required by provincial and/or federal law. They include Canada Pension Plan (CPP) contributions, Employment Insurance premiums, and personal income tax.

Canada Pension Plan (CPP). All employees between the ages of 18 and 70, whether self-employed or employed by others, must contribute to the CPP. Employees in Quebec contribute to the Quebec Pension Plan (QPP). Both plans give disability, retirement, and death benefits to qualifying Canadians.

Contribution rates are set by the federal government and are adjusted every January if there is an increase in the cost of living.

Employment Insurance (EI). The *Employment Insurance Act* requires all Canadian workers who are not self-employed to pay Employment Insurance (EI) premiums Employment insurance provides protection for a limited time period to employees who are temporarily laid off, who are on parental leave, or who lose their jobs.

Each year, the federal government determines the contribution rate and the maximum amount of premiums for the year.

Personal Income Tax. Employers must withhold income tax from employees each pay period in accordance with the *Income Tax Act*. The amount is determined by three variables: (1) the employee's gross pay, (2) the number of credits claimed by the employee, and (3) the length of the pay period.

There is no limit to the amount of gross pay that is subject to income tax withholdings. The higher the earnings, the higher the amount of taxes withheld. The best way to determine the amount of taxes that should be withheld is to use the payroll deduction tables supplied by the Canada Revenue Agency (CRA).

Voluntary Payroll Deductions. Unlike mandatory payroll deductions, which are required by law, voluntary payroll deductions are chosen by the employee. Employees may authorize withholdings for charitable, retirement, and other purposes. The employee must authorize these voluntary withholdings from gross earnings in writing. Deductions for union dues, extended health insurance, life insurance, and pension plans are often made on a group basis, while charitable deductions such as for the United Way are done individually.

Net Pay
The difference between an employee's gross pay, or total earnings, less any employee payroll deductions withheld from the earnings is known as net pay. This is the amount that the employer must pay to the employee.

Employer Payroll Costs

In addition to the initial expense for the total payroll (Wages and Salaries Expense), there are additional employer payroll costs. The federal government requires CPP and EI contributions from employers. The provincial governments requires employer funding of workplace health, safety, and compensation plans. These contributions, plus such items as paid vacations and pensions, are referred to as employee benefits. Employer payroll costs are not debited to the Salaries and Wages Expense account, but rather to a separate Employee Benefits Expense account.

Canada Pension Plan
Employers must also contribute to the CPP. For each dollar withheld from the employee's gross pay, the employer must contribute an equal amount. The CPP Payable account is credited for both the employees' and employer's CPP contributions.

Employment Insurance
Employers are required to contribute 1.4 times an employee's EI premiums. The EI Payable account is credited for both the employees' and employer's EI premiums.

Workplace Health, Safety, and Compensation
Workplace health, safety, and compensation plans give benefits to workers who are injured or disabled on the job. Employers must contribute to the plan at a rate based on risk of injury and past experience—usually between 0.25% and 10% of the gross payroll. The cost is paid entirely by the employer; there is no employee contribution.

Additional Employee Benefits
Employers incur other employee benefit costs for paid absences and post-employment benefits.

Paid Absences. Employers incur costs for employees for paid vacations, sick pay benefits, and paid holidays. Employees have the right to receive compensation for absences under certain conditions. When the liability for future paid absences can be estimated, it should be accrued. When it cannot be estimated, it should be disclosed in notes to the statements.

Post-Employment Benefits. Post-employment benefits are payments by employers to retired or terminated employees. These payments are for supplemental health and dental care, life insurance, and pensions. Employers must use the accrual basis in accounting for post-employment benefits. It is important to match the cost of these benefits with the periods when the employer benefits from the services of the employee.

Recording the Payroll

Recording the payroll involves maintaining payroll records, recording payroll expenses and liabilities, paying the payroll, and filing and remitting payroll deductions.

Payroll Records
Separate earnings records are kept for each employee and updated after each pay period. The **employee earnings record** provides a cumulative record of each employee's gross earnings, deductions, and net pay during the year. The employer uses this record to determine when an employee has reached the maximum earnings subject to CPP and EI premiums, to file information returns with the CRA, and to give each employee a statement of gross pay and withholdings for the year.

In addition to employee earnings records, many companies prepare a **payroll register** in which gross pay, deductions, and net pay per employee for each period are recorded. In other companies, the payroll register is a supplementary record that gives the data for a general journal entry and later posting to the ledger accounts.

Recording Payroll Expenses and Liabilities
Payroll costs are equal to the employees' gross salaries and wages plus the employer costs. Employee payroll deductions are collected by the employer and paid to the government or another third party. The deductions remain a current liability to the company until they are paid. Employee payroll costs and employer's payroll costs are typically recorded in separate journal entries.

Employee Payroll Costs

The typical journal entry to record a payroll is as follows:

Salaries Expense	XXX	
Wages Expense	XXX	
CPP Payable		XXX
EI Payable		XXX
Income Tax Payable		XXX
United Way Payable		XXX
Union Dues Payable		XXX
Salaries and Wages Payable		XXX

Employer Payroll Costs

Employer payroll costs include the matching amounts for CPP and EI, and the employers' amounts for workers' compensation plans and vacation pay. There may be other costs, like the health tax levied in Ontario, that would increase employer payroll costs.

The typical entry for recording payroll costs is as follows:

Employee Benefits Expense	XXX	
CPP Payable		XXX
EI Payable		XXX
Workers' Compensation Payable		XXX
Vacation Pay Payable		XXX

The liabilities are current liabilities since they will be paid within the next year. Employee Benefits Expense is sometimes combined with Salaries and Wages Expense on the income statement and is classified as an operating expense of the company.

Recording Payment of the Payroll

Payment of the payroll may be made by cheque or by electronic transfer of funds from the employer's bank account to the employee's bank account. A statement of earnings document that shows the employee's gross pay, payroll deductions, and net pay must accompany the cheques, or be given to the employee if the transfer is done electronically.

The entry to record the payroll payment is as follows:

Salaries and Wages Payable	XXX	
Cash		XXX

When companies report and remit their payroll deductions, they combine withholdings of income tax, CPP, and EI. Income tax, CPP, and EI must be reported and remitted monthly to the CRA on a Statement of Account for Current Source Deductions (Form PD7A) on or before the 15th day of the month following the payroll period. Depending on the size of the payroll deductions, however, the employer's payment deadline could be different.

Provincial workplace health, safety, and compensation plans require payments to be remitted quarterly. When payroll deductions are remitted, the accounting entry is as follows:

CPP Payable	XXX	
EI Payable	XXX	
Income Tax Payable	XXX	
United Way Payable	XXX	
Union Dues Payable	XXX	
Workers' Compensation Payable	XXX	
*Cash		XXX

*This cash payment is not a single cheque. CPP, EI, and income tax are paid to the government. United Way, union dues, and Workers' Compensation would be three separate cheques to different authorities.

At the end of each calendar year, a statement showing gross earnings, all payroll deductions, and income tax withheld for the year for each employee earnings is prepared. This information is reported to the CRA by the last day of February of the year following. The employer is required to provide each employee with a Statement of Remuneration Paid (Form T4) by the same date.

Financial Statement Presentation

Under Canadian GAAP for Private Enterprises, current liabilities are the first category reported in the liabilities section of the balance sheet. Each of the main types of current liabilities is listed separately. In addition, the terms of operating lines of credit and notes payable and other information about the individual items are disclosed in the notes to the financial statements.

> **Study objective 5**
> Prepare the current liabilities section of the balance sheet.

Current liabilities are usually listed in order of liquidity, by maturity date. Sometimes it is difficult to determine which specific obligations should be listed in which order. A more common method of presenting current liabilities is to list them by order of size, with the largest ones first. Many companies show bank loans, notes payable, and accounts payable first, regardless of the amounts.

Some companies reporting under IFRS may choose to order their current liability category on the lower section of the balance sheet, in order of reverse liquidity. Or they may choose to continue with the traditional placement of current liabilities as the first liability category on the balance sheet, in order of liquidity.

Companies must carefully monitor the relationship of current liabilities to current assets. The current ratio is calculated by dividing current assets by current liabilities. This relationship is critical in evaluating a company's short-term ability to pay debt. There is usually concern when a company has more current liabilities than current assets, because it may not be able to make its payments when they become due.

The current ratio should never be interpreted without also looking at the receivables and inventory turnover ratios to ensure that all of the current assets are indeed liquid. It is also important to look at the acid-test ratio.

APPENDIX 10A—Payroll Deductions

Study objective 6: Calculate mandatory payroll deductions.

Mandatory Payroll Deductions

Payroll deductions may be mandatory or voluntary. Mandatory deductions are required by law and include Canada Pension Plan contributions, Employment Insurance premiums, and income tax. We discuss how to calculate these in the following sections.

Canada Pension Plan (CPP)

CPP contributions are based on a maximum ceiling or limit (called the maximum pensionable earnings) less a basic yearly exemption, and the contribution rate set each year by the federal government. As of January 1, 2009, the following amounts were in effect:

Maximum pensionable earnings	$ 46,300
Basic yearly exemption	$ 3,500
CPP contribution rate	4.95%
Maximum annual employee CPP contribution	$2,118.60

Pensionable earnings are gross earnings less the basic yearly exemption.

Formula for CPP contributions

Step 1: Basic Yearly Exemption ÷ Number of Pay Periods in a Year = Basic Pay-Period Exemption

$3,500 ÷ 52 weeks in a year = $67.30 per week

Step 2: Employee's Gross Pay − Basic Pay-Period Exemption = Employee's Pensionable Earnings

$1,000.00 − $67.30 = $932.70

Step 3: Employee's Pensionable Earnings × CPP Contribution Rate = Employee's CPP Contribution

$932.70 × 4.95% = $46.17

An employer stops deducting CPP contributions if and when the employee's earnings are greater than the maximum pensionable earnings.

Employment Insurance (EI)

EI calculations are based on a maximum earnings ceiling (called the maximum annual insurable earnings) and the contribution rate set by the federal government each year. Different from CPP, there is no basic yearly exemption. For 2009, the following amounts were in effect:

Maximum insurable earnings	$42,300
EI contribution rate	1.73%
Maximum annual employee EI premium	$731.79

In most cases, **insurable earnings** are gross earnings.

The required EI premium is calculated by multiplying the employee's insurable earnings by the EI contribution rate.

Formula for EI premiums

$$\text{Employee's Insurable Earnings} \times \text{EI Contribution Rate} = \text{Employee's EI Premium}$$

$$\$1,000 \times 1.73\% = \$17.30$$

Personal Income Tax

Income tax deductions are based on income tax rates set by the federal and provincial governments. The federal government uses a progressive tax scheme when calculating income taxes. Basically, this means that the higher the pay or earnings, the higher the income tax percentage, and thus the higher the amount of taxes withheld. For example, effective April 1, 2009, the federal tax rates were the following:

- 15.5% on the first $41,200 of taxable income, plus
- 22% on the next $41,199 of taxable income (on the portion of taxable income between $41,200 and $82,399), plus
- 26% on the next $43,865 of taxable income (on the portion of taxable income between $82,399 and $126,264), plus
- 29% of taxable income over $126,264.

Taxable income is determined by the employee's gross pay and the amount of personal tax credits claimed by the employee. **Personal tax credits** are amounts deducted from an individual's income taxes and determine the amount of income taxes to be withheld. To indicate to the Canada Revenue Agency (CRA) which credits he or she wants to claim, the employee must complete a Personal Tax Credits Return (known as a TD1 form). In 2009, all individuals were entitled to a minimum personal credit (called the basic personal credit) of $10,375.

In addition, provincial income taxes must be calculated. All provinces, except Alberta, use a progressive tax scheme. Each province has its own specific tax rates and calculations.

The calculation of personal income tax deductions is very complicated. Consequently, it is best done using one of the many payroll accounting programs that are available or by using the payroll deduction tools provided by the CRA. These tools include (1) payroll deduction tables, (2) tables on diskette, and (3) the payroll deductions on-line calculator.

Using Payroll Deduction Tables

Payroll deduction tables are prepared by the CRA and can be easily downloaded from the CRA website at <http://www.cra-arc.gc.ca/tx/bsnss/tpcs/pyrll/menu-eng.html>. There are separate payroll deduction tables for determining federal tax deductions, provincial tax deductions, Canada Pension Plan contributions, and Employment Insurance premiums.

These tables are updated at least once a year on January 1 to reflect the new rates for that year. Income tax tables are also reissued during the year if the federal or provincial governments make changes to income tax rates during the year. It is important to make sure you have the tables that are in effect during the payroll period for which you are calculating deductions.

There are separate sections of the federal and provincial income tax and the CPP tables for weekly, biweekly, semi-monthly, and monthly pay periods. Thus, when determining these amounts it is important to make sure you are using the table prepared for the company's pay period.

Demonstration Problem (SO 1, 2 and 4)

The following are selected transactions of the Cascade Costume Company during February and March 2011:

Feb. 10 Sales on credit for the period February 1–10 totalled $100,000. 5% GST and 8% PST were added to sales.

Feb. 16 Based on experience, it is estimated that the cost of the product warranty liability will be approximately 5% of the sales for the month. The company set up the liability for warranty expense. The company expects total sales for the month to be $300,000.

Feb. 18 Items under warranty were repaired. Costs for labour and repair parts were in the amount of $300.

Feb. 28 Wages to four new employees in the amount of $2,600 were calculated to February 28. The total amounts withheld were income tax $425.00, CPP $116.50, and EI $48.62. The company's matched contributions were for CPP (1 time) and EI (1.4 times). The employer benefit costs were also recorded.

Feb. 28 Wages were paid to employees.

Feb. 28 A $15,000, two-month, 10% note payable signed on December 31, 2010, was paid off. Interest had been accrued to January 31, 2011.

Mar. 15 Withholdings from employees were paid to the government agency.

Solution to Demonstration Problem

General Journal			J1
Date	Account Titles and Explanation	Debit	Credit
2011			
Feb. 10	Accounts Receivable	113,000.00	
	GST Payable		5,000.00
	PST Payable		8,000.00
	Sales		100,000.00
	To record sales and sales taxes payable.		
Feb. 16	Warranty Expense	15,000.00	
	Warranty Liability		15,000.00
	To accrue estimated warranty costs.		
	($300,000 × 5%)		
Feb. 18	Warranty Liability	300.00	
	Repair Parts Inventory, Wages Payable		300.00
	To honour warranty contracts to date.		
Feb. 28	Wages Expense	2,600.00	
	Income Tax Payable		425.00
	CPP Payable		116.50

		EI Payable		48.62
		Wages Payable		2,009.88
		To record wages payable.		
		Employee Benefits Expense	184.57	
		CPP Payable		116.50
		EI Payable ($48.62 × 1.4)		68.07
		To record employee benefit costs to date.		
Feb. 28	Wages Payable	2,009.88	
	Cash		2,009.88
	To record payment of wages.		
Feb. 28	Notes Payable	15,000.00	
	Interest Payable	125.00	
	Interest Expense	125.00	
	Cash		15,250.00
	To record payment of Notes Payable with accrued interest and current interest expense.		
Mar. 15	Income Tax Payable	425.00	
	CPP Payable ($116.50 + $116.50)	233.00	
	EI Payable ($48.62 + $68.07)	116.69	
	Cash		774.69
	To record payment of withholdings and employee benefit costs.		

Review Questions and Exercises

Multiple Choice

Circle the letter that best answers each of the following statements.

1. (SO 1) Which of the following statements concerning liabilities is incorrect?
   a. A liability occurs as a result of present obligations.
   b. A liability arises from a past event.
   c. Liabilities include prepaid expenses.
   d. A liability is an obligation to make future payments of assets or services.

Questions 2 and 3 pertain to the following information: On October 1, 2011, DeHaviland Company issued a $28,000, nine-month, 10% note.

2. (SO 1) If DeHaviland Company is preparing financial statements at December 31, 2011, the adjusting entry for accrued interest will include:
   a. credit to Notes Payable of $700.
   b. debit to Interest Expense of $700.

c. credit to Interest Payable of $2,100.
d. debit to Interest Expense of $2,800.

3. (SO 1) Assuming interest was accrued on June 30, 2012, the entry to record the payment of the note will include a:

    a. debit to Interest Expense of $700.
    b. credit to Cash of $28,000.
    c. debit to Interest Payable of $2,100.
    d. debit to Notes Payable of $30,100.

4. (SO 1) On August 1, 2011, a company borrowed cash and signed a one-year, interest-bearing note that matures on August 1, 2012. How will the note payable and the related interest be classified in the December 31, 2011, balance sheet?

	Note Payable	**Interest Payable**
a.	Current liability	Non-current liability
b.	Non-current liability	Current liability
c.	Current liability	Current liability
d.	Long-term liability	Not shown

5. (SO 1) Travis Company has total proceeds from sales, including GST, of $21,000. If the GST is 5%, the amount to be credited to the Sales account is:

    a. $21,000.
    b. $19,900.
    c. $19,000.
    d. $20,000.

6. (SO 1) An operating line of credit has the following features except:

    a. it is pre-authorized by the bank.
    b. it helps companies manage temporary cash shortfalls.
    c. it does not have a pre-set limit.
    d. it enables timely payments of current liabilities.

7. (SO 1) Money borrowed through a line of credit:

    a. is normally borrowed on a short-term basis.
    b. is repayable at any time when the company has money.
    c. covers any and all cheques written by the company.
    d. is usually demanded by the bank without notice.

Use the following information to answer questions 8 and 9: During 2011, Preston Company sells 1,200 products at $10 each. The products are sold with a one-year warranty. Preston estimates that 12% of the units sold will be returned under warranty and repaired at an average of $3 per unit. During 2011, 108 units are repaired under warranty at an average of $3 per unit. The balance in Preston Company's Warranty Liability account at January 1, 2011, is $380 (credit).

8. (SO 2) The amount of warranty expense that Preston Company should report for 2011 is:
   a. $1,440.
   b. $144.
   c. $324.
   d. $432.

9. (SO 2) The balance in the Warranty Liability account at December 31, 2011, is:
   a. $380.
   b. $488.
   c. $1,136.
   d. $704.

10. (SO 2) All of the following statements about customer loyalty programs are true except:
    a. companies offer customer loyalty programs to attract and keep customers.
    b. companies expect customer loyalty programs to increase sales.
    c. customer loyalty programs result in an estimated liability.
    d. customer loyalty programs are recorded as an increase in expense.

11. (SO 2) In September 2011, the Lucky Company issued 500 redemption rewards, which would save customers $0.50 on each $10.00 of groceries purchased. By December 31, 2011, 300 redemption rewards had been redeemed. The balance in the account Redemption Reward Liability account is:
    a. $250.
    b. $5,000.
    c. $100.
    d. $150.

12. (SO 3) How should an estimated loss be handled if it is reasonably likely and the amount can be reasonably estimated?

	Accrued	Disclosed
a.	Yes	No
b.	No	Yes
c.	Yes	Yes
d.	No	No

13. (SO 3) Under IFRS, a contingent liability is disclosed in all of the following circumstances except when:
    a. a possible (but not likely) obligation exists but will be confirmed only by the occurrence or non-occurrence of an uncertain future event.
    b. the probability of occurrence is remote.
    c. a present obligation exists but it is not probable that the company will have to settle it.
    d. a present obligation exists but the amount cannot be reliably measured.

14. (SO 3) Under Canadian GAAP for Private Enterprises, a contingent liability would be recorded under the following conditions:

    a. The contingency is likely (the chance of occurrence is high).
    b. The probability of occurrence is remote.
    c. The amount of the contingency can be reasonably estimated.
    d. Both a and c.

15. (SO 3) Which of the following statements about contingent assets is not true?

    a. They involve uncertainty that will be resolved in the future.
    b. An example is a legal action that could favour the company.
    c. They are never recorded or accrued in the financial statements.
    d. They are never disclosed under any circumstance.

16. (SO 3) Contingent assets are disclosed when they are likely and reasonably estimable but never recorded because:

    a. this is the same way contingent liabilities are treated.
    b. it is likely that gains may not be realized by the company.
    c. of the conservative nature of accounting.
    d. it is impossible to estimate the exact amount of the asset.

17. (SO 4) Payroll accounting involves all of the following except:

    a. paying salary and wages.
    b. reporting and remitting payroll deductions.
    c. interviewing and hiring employees.
    d. having payroll records for each employee.

18. (SO 4) Accounting for employee payroll costs involves calculating:

    a. gross pay.
    b. net pay.
    c. payroll deductions.
    d. all of the above.

19. (SO 4) Jan Turner earns $16 per hour for a 40-hour work week and $24 per hour for overtime work. If Turner works 44 hours, and overtime payment is 1.5 times regular hourly wages, her gross weekly earnings are:

    a. $704.
    b. $736.
    c. $836.
    d. $1,056.

20. (SO 4) The journal entry to record the payroll for Garvey Company for the week ending January 8, would probably include a:

    a. credit to Office Salaries.
    b. credit to Wages Expense.
    c. debit to Income Tax Payable.
    d. credit to CPP Payable.

21. (SO 5) Under Canadian GAAP for Private Enterprises, which of the following is not true regarding current liabilities?

    a. They are the first category reported in the liabilities section of the balance sheet.
    b. The main types of current liabilities are listed together.
    c. They are usually listed in order of liquidity, by maturity date.
    d. The terms of operating lines of credit and notes payable are disclosed in the notes to the financial statements.

22. (SO 5) The current ratio is:

    a. an indicator of a company's long-term ability to pay debt.
    b. calculated by dividing current liabilities by current assets.
    c. calculated by dividing current assets by current liabilities.
    d. is a concern when a company has more current assets than current liabilities.

*23. (SO 6) Which of the following would not be classified as a mandatory payroll deduction for employees?

    a. Canada Pension Plan contributions
    b. Employment Insurance premiums
    c. Personal income tax
    d. Workers' compensation deductions

*24. (SO 6) Lewis Latimer, an employee of Southam Company, has gross earnings for the month of October of $4,000. CPP is 4.95% of gross earnings, EI premium is 1.73% of gross earnings, income tax amounts to $1,072 for the month, and Lewis authorizes voluntary deductions of $10 per month for the United Way. The company must match the CPP deduction and pay 1.4 times the EI premium. What is the net pay for Lewis Latimer?

    a. $2,452.20
    b. $2,342.80
    c. $2,650.80
    d. $2,918.00

Matching

Match each term with its definition by writing the appropriate letter in the space provided.

Terms	Definitions
___ 1. Customer loyalty programs	a. Payments made by an employer, in addition to wages and salaries, to give pension, insurance, medical, or other benefits to its employees.
___ 2. Notes payable	b. Deductions required by law that include income tax, Canada Pension Plan contributions, and Employment Insurance premiums.
___ 3. Contingent liability	c. Promises made by the seller to a buyer to repair or replace a product if it is defective or does not perform as intended.

___ 4. Employee benefits   d. A present obligation exists but the amount cannot be reliably measured.

___ 5. Contingent assets   e. Amounts withheld from gross pay to determine the amount of net pay due to an employee.

___ 6. Mandatory payroll deductions   f. Include insurance claims or potential legal actions that could favour the company.

___ 7. Product warranties   g. Obligations in the form of written promissory notes.

___ 8. Payroll deductions   h. Cash rebates, coupons, or other items offered as a decrease in sales price to encourage sales.

Exercises

E10—1 (SO 1) The following transactions took place during 2011 for Reel Pots and Pans Company:

Aug. 1 Borrowed $10,000 cash from the Hong Kong Bank by issuing a $10,000, eight-month, 9% note. Interest is payable at maturity.

Oct. 1 Borrowed $18,000 cash from the First Financial Credit Union by issuing a three-month, 10% note. Interest is payable the first of each month starting November 1.

Nov. 1 Paid one month's interest on the October 1 note.

Dec. 1 Paid one month's interest on the October 1 note.

Dec. 24 Determined from cash register readings that sales were $27,120 with the GST (5%) and PST (8%) included.

Instructions
a. Journalize the transactions above.
b. Prepare the adjusting entries for the two notes at December 31, 2011.
c. Record the payment of the two notes in 2012 at their maturity dates.

General Journal			J1
Date	**Account Titles and Explanation**	**Debit**	**Credit**
2011			
a.			

b.			
c.			

E10—2 (SO 1) Coast Industries received its annual property tax bill for $22,200 on May 1, payable June 30. Coast has a December 31 fiscal year end and makes annual adjusting entries.

Instructions
a. Prepare the journal entry to record the receipt of the property tax bill on May 1.
b. Prepare the journal entry to record the payment of the property tax bill June 30.
c. Prepare any adjusting entries required at December 31.

General Journal			J1
Date	Account Titles and Explanation	Debit	Credit
2011			
a.			
b.			
c.			

E10—3 (SO 2) Robins Wireless sells cell phones with a 120-day warranty for defective merchandise. Based on past experience Robins estimates 2% of the units sold will become defective in the warranty period. Management estimates that repair costs will average $20 per unit. The units sold and actual units defective in the first two months of 2011 are as follows:

Month	Units Sold	Units Defective	Actual Repair Cost
January	15,000	150	$3,000
February	16,000	210	$4,200

Instructions
a. Prepare journal entries to record the estimated liability costs on January 31 and February 28.
b. Prepare journal entries to record the repair of the defective units.

General Journal			J1
Date	Account Titles and Explanation	Debit	Credit
2011			
a.			

b.			

E10—4 (SO 2) In September 2011, Beautique Skin Care Company sold 10,000 packages of its newly formulated skin cleanser. Each package included a $4 gift certificate.

Beautique estimates that 80% of the purchasers will use the gift certificate.

By December 31, 2011, 1,500 customers had redeemed their gift certificate.

Instructions
a. Prepare an entry to record the estimated gift certificate liability as of September 30, 2011.
b. Prepare an entry to record the redeemed gift certificates at the end of December 31, 2011.

General Journal			J1
Date	Account Titles and Explanation	Debit	Credit
2011			
a.			

b.			

*E10—5(SO 4 & 6) The following information pertains to the payroll of B. T. MacDonald Company for the week ended January 21, 2011. All hours over 44 are paid at one and one-half times the regular hourly rate.

Employee	Total Hours Worked	Hourly Rate	Income Tax	United Way	Union Dues
E. Bouchet	45	$13.00	$110	$10	$5
C. Cullen	44	15.00	138	12	5
M. Henson	38	10.00	64	10	5
B. Mays	48	12.00	100	14	5

Instructions

a. Complete the schedule below. CPP is 4.95% of gross earnings, and EI is 1.73% of gross earnings.
b. Prepare the entry to record the payroll on January 21.
c. Prepare the journal entry to record payment of the payroll on January 28.
d. Record the employer's payroll costs, assuming employers must match employees' CPP and pay 1.4 times the employees' EI.
e. Record the payment of payroll withholdings to the Receiver General on February 15.

a.

	Gross Earnings	CPP	EI	Income Tax	United Way	Union Dues	Net Pay
E. Bouchet							
C. Cullen							
M. Henson							
B. Mays							
Totals							

Chapter 10: Current Liabilities and Payroll 329

Date	General Journal Account Titles and Explanation	Debit	J1 Credit
2011			
b.			
c.			
d.			
e.			

Solutions to Review Questions and Exercises

Multiple Choice

1. (c) Prepaid expenses are current assets. Answers (a), (b), and (d) are all correct statements.

2. (b) The adjusting entry for the company is as follows:

Interest Expense	700	
Interest Payable		700

    ($28,000 × 10% × 3/12)

3. (c) The entry to record the payment of the note is as follows:

Notes Payable	28,000	
Interest Payable	2,100	
Cash		30,100

4. (c) Because the note and the accrued interest are payable within one year from December 31, 2011, they should both be classified as current liabilities.

5. (d) The entry for Travis Company to record sales and sales taxes is as follows:

Cash	21,000	
Sales ($21,000/105%)		20,000
GST Payable ($20,000 × 5%)		1,000

6. (c) An operating line of credit is pre-authorized by the bank so a company can borrow money when needed up to a pre-set limit.

7. (a) A line of credit makes it easy for a company to borrow on a short-term basis.

8. (d) The amount of warranty expense to report for the year is based on the estimated number of units to be repaired (1,200 × 12% = 144), multiplied by the average estimated cost to repair each unit (144 × $3 = $432).

9. (b) The new balance in the estimated warranty liability account is the opening balance ($380), plus the estimated warranty expense for the year ($432), minus the actual warranty claims made during the year (108 × $3 = $324).

10. (d) Customer loyalty programs are accounted for as a decrease in revenue not as an expense.

11. (c) The Lucky Company has 500 redemption rewards that would be redeemed so the Redemption Reward Liability account would have a credit balance of $250 (500 × .50). The 300 redemption rewards redeemed by December 2011 would be (300 × $0.50) $150, which would be debited to the account. Thus, the balance in the account would be $100.

12. (c) When a contingency is likely and the amount reasonably estimable, the liability should be recorded in the accounts. When a contingency does not meet the

13. (b) Contingent liabilities are disclosed only in the notes to the financial statements, unless the probability of occurrence is remote. (a), (c) and (d) are correct.

14. (d) Both (a) and (c) are correct. The contingency is likely (the chance of occurrence is high). The amount of the contingency can be reasonably estimated.

15. (d) Contingent assets (gains) are disclosed when they are likely and are reasonably estimable and also when they are likely but not estimable.

16. (c) The goal of conservatism is to be sure that any negative effect on investors and creditors be fully disclosed but not recorded.

17. (c) Payroll accounting performs (a), (b), and (d) but is not responsible for interviewing and hiring employees. The human resource department typically does that.

18. (d) Accounting for employee payroll costs involves calculating (a) gross pay, (b) payroll deductions, and (c) net pay.

19. (a) Gross earnings are $704. (Regular 44 × $16 = $704). Overtime premiums are not paid until the employee has worked more than 44 hours in a seven-day period.

20. (d) An example of a typical payroll entry is as follows:

Office Salaries Expense	XXXX	
Wages Expense	XXXX	
CPP (or QPP) Payable		XXXX
Income Tax Payable		XXXX
EI Payable		XXXX
United Way Payable		XXXX
Salaries and Wages Payable		XXXX

21. (b) The main types of current liabilities are listed separately.

22. (c) Calculated by dividing current assets by current liabilities.

*23. (d) Workers' Compensation deductions are costs that the employer must pay.

*24. (c) The net pay is calculated as follows:

Gross earnings		$4,000.00
Payroll deductions:		
Employment Insurance ($4,000 × 1.73%)	$ 69.20	
Income tax	1,072.00	
Canada Pension Plan ($4,000 × 4.95%)	198.00	
United Way	10.00	1,349.20
Net pay		$2,650.80

Matching

1. h   4. a   7. c
2. g   5. f   8. e
3. d   6. b

Exercises

E10—1

General Journal			J1
Date	Account Titles and Explanation	Debit	Credit
2011			
a.			
Aug. 1	Cash	10,000	
	Notes Payable		10,000
	To record issue of $10,000, eight-month, 9% note.		
Oct. 1	Cash	18,000	
	Notes Payable		18,000
	To record issue of $18,000, three-month, 10% note.		
Nov. 1	Interest Expense	150	
	Cash		150
	To pay one month interest on Oct. 1 note. ($18,000 × 10% × 1/12)		
Dec. 1	Interest Expense	150	
	Cash		150
	To pay one month interest on Oct. 1 note. ($18,000 × 10% × 1/12)		
Dec. 24	Cash	27,120	
	Sales ($27,120 ÷ 1.13)		24,000
	GST Payable ($24,000 × 5%)		1,200
	PST Payable ($24,000 × 8%)		1,920
	To record daily sales and sales taxes.		
b.			
Dec. 31	Interest Expense	375	
	Interest Payable		375
	To record interest expense for five months. ($10,000 × 9% × 5/12)		
31	Interest Expense	150	
	Interest Payable		150
	To record interest expense for one month. ($18,000 × 10% × 1/12)		

c.

Date	Account Titles	Debit	Credit
2012			
Jan. 1	Notes Payable	18,000	
	Interest Payable	150	
	Cash		18,150
	To record payment of First Financial Credit Union note and accrued interest.		
Mar. 31	Interest Expense	225	
	Interest Payable		225
	To record interest expense for three months. ($10,000 × 9% × 3/12)		
Mar. 31	Notes Payable	10,000	
	Interest Payable	600	
	Cash		10,600
	To record payment of Hong Kong bank note with accrued interest.		

E10—2

	General Journal		J1
Date	Account Titles	Debit	Credit
2011			
a.			
May 1	Property Tax Expense	7,400	
	Property Tax Payable		7,400
	($22,200 × 4/12)		
b.			
Jun. 30	Property Tax Expense*	3,700	
	Property Tax Payable	7,400	
	Prepaid Property Taxes**	11,100	
	Cash		22,200
	*($22,200 × 2/12) = $3,700 **($22,200 × 6/12) = $11,100		
c.			
Dec. 31	Property Tax Expense	11,100	
	Prepaid Property Taxes		11,100

E10—3

	General Journal		J1
Date	Account Titles	Debit	Credit
a.			
Jan. 31	Warranty Expense	6,000	
	Warranty Liability		6,000
	To accrue estimated warranty liability. (15,000 × 2% × $20)		
Feb. 28	Warranty Expense	6,400	
	Warranty Liability		6,400
	To accrue estimated warranty liability. (16,000 × 2% × $20)		
b.			
Jan. 31	Warranty Liability	3,000	
	Repair Parts (and/or Wages Payable)		3,000
	To record honouring of 150 warranties.		
Feb. 28	Warranty Liability	4,200	
	Repair Parts (and/or Wages Payable)		4,200
	To record honouring of 210 warranties.		

E10—4

	General Journal		J1
Date	Account Titles and Explanation	Debit	Credit
a.			
Sep. 30	Sales Discount for Gift Certificate Redemption	32,000	
	Gift Certificate Liability		32,000
	To accrue estimated gift certificate liability.		
	(10,000 × 80% × $4)		
b.			
Dec. 31	Gift Certificate Liability	6,000	
	Cash		6,000
	To record redemption of certificates. (1,500 × $4)		

*E10—5

a.

	Gross Earnings	CPP	EI	Income Tax	United Way	Union Dues	Net Pay
E. Bouchet	$ 591.50	$ 29.28	$10.23	$110.00	$10.00	$ 5.00	$ 426.99
C. Cullen	660.00	32.67	11.42	138.00	12.00	5.00	460.91
M. Henson	380.00	18.81	6.57	64.00	10.00	5.00	275.62
B. Mays	600.00	29.70	10.38	100.00	14.00	5.00	440.92
Totals	$2,231.50	$110.46	$38.60	$412.00	$46.00	$20.00	$1,604.44

General Journal			J1
Date	Account Titles and Explanation	Debit	Credit
2011			
b.			
Jan. 21	Wages Expense	2,231.50	
	CPP Payable		110.46
	EI Payable		38.60
	Income Tax Payable		412.00
	United Way Payable		46.00
	Union Dues Payable		20.00
	Wages Payable		1,604.44
	To record payroll for the week ending January 21.		
c.			
Jan. 28	Wages Payable	1,604.44	
	Cash		1,604.44
	To record payment of January 21 payroll.		
d.			
Jan. 28	Employee Benefits Expense	164.50	
	CPP Payable		110.46
	EI Payable		54.04
	To record employer payroll cost on January 21.		
e.			
Feb. 15	Income Tax Payable	412.00	
	CPP Payable	220.92	
	EI Payable	92.64	
	Cash		725.56
	To record payment to the Receiver General for January payroll.		